THE CAT-FLAP AND THE APPLE PIE
AND OTHER FUNNY STORIES

THE CAT-FLAP AND THE APPLE PIE

AND OTHER FUNNY STORIES

by
Joan Aiken, Christianna Brand,
Helen Cresswell, Marjorie Darke,
Dorothy Edwards, Diana Wynne Jones,
Gene Kemp and Ursula Moray Williams

Compiled by Lance Salway

Illustrated by Jill Bennett

A Children's Book from
W. H. ALLEN · LONDON
A Howard & Wyndham Company
1979

Printed and bound in Great Britain by
Billing & Sons Ltd., Guildford, Worcester & London,
for the Publishers, W. H. Allen & Co. Ltd,
44 Hill Street, London W1X 8LB

ISBN 0 491 02385 5

Contents

The Cat-Flap and the Apple Pie

Joan Aiken

It was the last day of the summer holidays. Apples lay about all over the grass. A burnt patch on the lawn showed where the boys had had a bonfire, the week before, and cooked sausages. Wet sandy swimming trunks hung on the clothes line, and several dozen sea-shells were strewn over the front path, where somebody had dropped them and somebody else had kicked them.

The Crask family were having breakfast. Tim Crask had already eaten his, and was cramming bread and cheese into his anorak pockets.

'I'm going down to Beezeley's farm to drive the tractor,' he said. 'Shan't be back till supper time.'

'It's illegal to drive a tractor at your age,' said Mr Crask, with his head in the newspaper. He had been saying this all through the holidays.

'I'm driving it in a field, not on the road,' said Tim, as he had all through the holidays.

'Mind you get back in time to put your things together for school,' said Mrs Crask. 'Have you done your holiday work?'

Tim took no notice of this.

'There's a horrible draught coming from the back door,' said Mr Crask. 'Can somebody shut it?'

'Mishkin's outside.'

'For heaven's sake! Can't that kitten learn to miaow, if he wants to come in?'

'Nobody hears him. And that big fat black tom of the Kingsleys chases him — he hasn't got *time* to miaow.'

'Well, leave the scullery window open.'

'Then the Kingsleys' cat comes in and beats him up in here.'

'I wish we'd never *got* that cat,' Mr Crask said from inside his paper.

The phone rang.

'Answer it, will you, Tim, there's a love, as you're standing up,' said Mrs Crask, who was washing twenty jampots preparatory to making blackberry-and-apple jelly.

Tim scowled, but answered the phone, which was in the hall.

'It's Aunt Daphne, wanting to speak to Dad,' he said returning with an expressionless face.

Mr Crask went into the hall.

'Hullo, Daphne,' they heard him say. 'Oh — are you? Yes, that would be perfectly okay. No, we aren't — good to see you all. What time will you get here? Yes, yes, we're all here — school starts tomorrow. Fine — see you, then.'

Mr Crask's telephone conversations never lasted long. He came back into the kitchen, having hardly stopped reading his paper, which he carried with him, and sat down again.

'Daphne and Bob and the girls are coming to lunch,' he announced, looking over the top for a moment.

'*What?*' shrieked his wife.

George's face assumed an expression of settled

despair. Tim walked quietly out of the house, mounted his bike and rode off.

'*Tim!* Come back!'

No good. Tim was already out of earshot.

'You *asked* them to *lunch* — when you know I've got all the boys' school clothes to go through — and I was going to make blackberry jelly — '

'They asked themselves. They said they were driving by this way. What else could I do?'

'*I* shan't talk to those horrible girls,' George said. 'All they can do is brag about their school and how well they did in their O-levels.'

'You certainly *will* talk to them,' said his father. 'It's very rude not to. What will you give them for lunch, Ann?'

Mrs Crask looked distraught. 'George, do you think you could cycle down to the butcher and get some steak-and-kidney? Then I suppose I could make a stew.'

'Stew! That's not very festive.'

'I don't feel very festive,' said Mrs Crask flatly.

'Yes, I'll go,' said George, who liked stew. 'Then I can get a cat-flap at Moxon's, and put it in the back door.'

'*I'm* not paying for any cat-flap,' said Mr Crask.

'I've got enough money myself. From potato-lifting,' said George.

'Well, don't come running to *me* when you've made a mess of it,' said his father. George didn't answer that one.

Breakfast was over. Mr Crask strolled out to finish reading his paper in the garden, as the weather was so fine and warm. Mrs Crask looked round the house, which was a total mess. A lot of left-over picnic things had been dumped in the hall. The dining room had been used for a game of Progressive Pingpong, with obstacles piled up around the table to make it harder for the players to run from one end to the other. The sitting room had a lot of deckchairs in it because it had come on to rain suddenly last night and it was quicker to bring the chairs in than take them all the way down to the shed.

'We'll have to tidy the house,' Mrs Crask said to George when he came back with the meat and the cat-flap.

'I want to fix this in the back door. Look,' said George, as Mishkin, the marmalade kitten, shot across the lawn, pursued by the fat black tom from next door.

George rushed out and aimed a swipe at the black tom with a cricket bat, but missed him and chopped the heads off a clump of marigolds. Mishkin came indoors wailing and wanting to be picked up and petted. One of his ears was covered in blood. George took the cat-flap out of its wrappings.

'Tidy the house *first,* before you start on the cat-flap,' his mother said.

George gloomily helped her.

'It's unfair that Tim gets out of this,' he said.

It was unfair, and his mother knew it.

'Life is unfair,' she said. 'It's unfair that I have to make lunch for the Bewdleys when I want to get on with my jam.'

'I *hate* those girls,' said George. 'Susan wears lipstick. *Lipstick!* Ugh.'

'What are you going to give them for afters?' Mr Crask shouted from the front garden.

'They can have bread and cheese and fruit, as we've done all holidays.'

'They most certainly can *not!* Why don't you make them an apple pie; Daphne loves your orange-flavoured apple pies. Yes,' said Mr Crask, 'make them an apple pie.'

'Oh, *fudge,*' muttered Mrs Crask.

Dashing about, she and George tidied the dining room and the sitting room, hurling everything into the cupboard under the stairs.

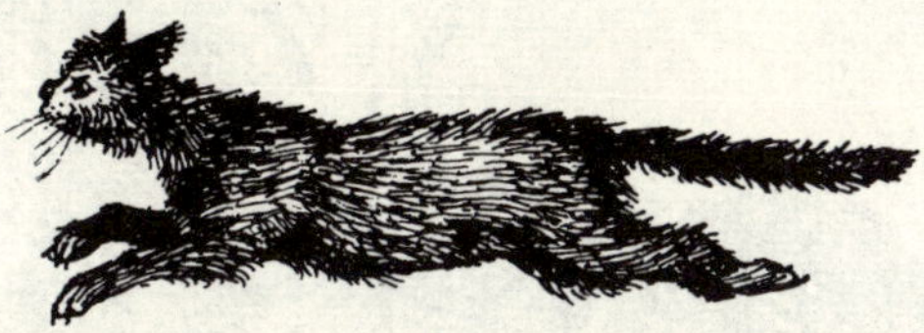

The stew was begun, and put on to simmer. George scrubbed a lot of potatoes ready for baking.

Then he got a fretsaw and cut an oblong out of the back door, the same size as the cat-flap that he had bought. The job was hideously difficult, because the back door was made of hard, weathered boards, very likely fifty years old. Also, his mother kept interrupting him.

'George, could you go and pick me some parsley and thyme. George, could you be a love and take this basket and get some runner-beans, enough for seven people.'

'It's like eating walking sticks,' grumbled George, returning with the basket of enormous, tough, stringy beans. As he shut the back door the fat black tom from the next house jumped in through the hole he had just sawed. *'Get out!'* said George, furiously swatting it with the basket. Beans flew about the kitchen.

Mrs Crask let out a sudden shriek.

'*Now* what's the matter, Mum?'

'I put the orange for the apple pie into the oven to soften up, and forgot all about it. Now it's gone all brown and hard.'

'Pour boiling water on it,' suggested George, looking at the pie-dish of cut-up orange pieces; they had turned mahogany-brown.

'But that would dilute the orange flavour,' objected his mother.

'Pour on some orange squash then.'

'No — I know — I'll soak them in sherry.'

'*That's* not orange flavour.'

'No, but it's fairly like. And doesn't taste so phoney as orange squash. And then I'll put them back in the oven, just for a minute or two, to soften up again. *Don't let me forget they're in the oven.* Oh, George, could you be an *angel* and go and pick up some windfall apples. Enough to make a pie.'

While George was picking up the apples, the phone rang.

'Could you answer it, Andrew,' called Mrs Crask to her husband. 'My hands are all covered in pastry.'

'*Never* get a *minute* to read the *paper,*' grumbled Mr Crask, coming into the hall. He snatched up the receiver. 'Yes, who is it? Oh, Daphne, you again — what is it now?'

George, returning with the apples, met his mother's eyes.

'Perhaps they can't come after all,' she whispered hopefully.

'Oh, Andrew, dear,' said Mr Crask's sister at the other end. 'Look, it seems the girls invited their friend Felicity for the day. Will it be all right if we bring her along too?'

'Oh sure. Two or three, four or five, what's the

difference?' said Mr Crask heartily. 'See you then. 'Bye.'

'The girls are bringing that friend of theirs, too,' he shouted through the kitchen door. 'Lord, this room's a mess! I hope you tidy it up before they come.'

He returned to his paper.

'Oh, not that *awful Felicity!*' said George, aghast. 'I cannot *stand* it! Well, I'm certainly not going to talk to *her.*'

'George, you must. I'm sorry, but you must. Oh, *damn*-my bits of orange!'

Mrs Crask leapt to the oven.

The orange pulp had now cooked to a dark-brown goo, but the slices of peel were still as tough as oak bark.

'If I were you, I should just use the goo, and throw away the peel,' said George.

'There won't be enough goo to flavour the pie, without the peel.'

'Well, mash it all up with the little mixer, then. I'll do that if you like,' said George, who was rather fond of using the little mixer. It was a single electric prong with a tiny fierce windmill at its tip; you had to be very careful when using it, for if the windmill part came above the surface of whatever you were mixing, splashes shot all over the room.

Indeed, it proved to be a mistake to use it on the baked cut-up orange. The blades of the windmill kept encountering hard bits of orange peel, and the kitchen was soon generously spattered with dark-brown gooey splashes.

'Stop, *stop!*' shouted Mrs Crask. 'You are wasting all my orange on the walls.'

'Well, you'd better put it in the big blender, then,' advised George.

'There's hardly any left,' said Mrs Crask, looking into the bottom of the dish.

'Add some more sherry to it.'

Even so, Mrs Crask had to keep tilting the big blender from side to side, or the blades went round uselessly, without finding anything to mince up.

'All this for an apple pie for those brutes to eat!' said George, and he went back to work on his cat-flap. The flap came in two parts, a frame, which fitted into the hole he had cut, and a hinged door, which slotted into the frame. At this point George realised that he had put the frame in upside down. While he was reversing it, the fat black tom from next door chased Mishkin through the hole. Mishkin fled screaming and knocked over the pot of glue that George had been using. George grabbed a ratchet screwdriver and aimed a swipe at the black tom, just missing him. As he had picked up the screwdriver by the blade part, he cut his hand quite deeply, but did not notice this until he began to wonder where all the blood on the floor was coming from.

Mishkin sat on top of the broom cupboard, wailing.

The phone rang again.

'Someone *else* will have to get it *this* time,' said Mr Crask. 'I'm just going for some cigarettes. *Good God,* what a mess,' he said, looking at the floor inside the back door, which was covered with glue, sawdust, wood-splinters, blood, and tools. 'I hope you'll have the kindness to get that cleared up before they come.'

George answered the phone, covering the receiver with blood and glue.

'Oh, hullo, Aunt Daphne. Yes. I see. You want to get here at twelve, for an early lunch, because the girls want to go on to the beach afterwards. Yes. Okay. Goodbye,' said George tonelessly, and he said to his mother, who was peering into the blender, 'They want to get here at twelve for an early lunch.'

His mother did not reply.

'What are you going to give them for starters?' said Mr Crask from the doorway.

'Andrew! Daphne is your *sister!* The Bewdleys do *not* rate *hors-d'oeuvres.'*

'Well, I'd have thought you could give them *something.* Stuffed tomatoes or *something,'* said Mr Crask as he went up the front path, kicking the heap of shells out of his way.

George washed his hands, stuck a plaster on the worst of the cuts, and slotted the cat-flap into its frame.

Mrs Crask cut up the windfall apples and put them in a pie-dish.

The sky clouded over and a light rain started to fall.

'They won't want to go to the beach in this,' said Mrs Crask, looking out.

'Oh, heavens! We'll have them for the whole afternoon!' groaned George.

There was a sudden outburst of screeching and caterwauling from the garden. The fat black tom shot through George's new cat-flap, pursued by the tough tabby from three houses along.

The house seemed full of cats. They went skittering upstairs.

'Where's Mishkin?' said Mrs Crask.

Mishkin was outside the cat-flap, wailing pitifully. He did not know how to use it.

'Look, you dumb oaf, you do it like this,' George told him. 'Put your nose under the flap and *tip* it *up.'*

He demonstrated over and over, he held Mishkin up to the flap, he pushed him through, he pulled him through. Mishkin still totally failed to grasp the principle.

'Try cutting a slit in a cork and sticking it on the side of the flap to hold it open,' suggested Mrs Crask. 'I've heard that helps. Oh, *heavens,* my stew!'

She snatched it off the stove.

'Has it dried up?'

'A bit. Not too bad.'

'Put some orange squash in it,' suggested George, slicing a cork with a razorblade. The fat black tom bolted past him, making its getaway, and he cut his thumb.

Mishkin sat inside the cat-flap and wailed.

'I'm fed up!' said George suddenly. 'I'm going to turn into a tree.'

He went out on to the damp front lawn. From his trouser pocket he took a small tube of water. He poured some of the water on to his shoes.

'George!' shouted his mother through the window. 'Don't be silly!'

George took no notice.

He stood motionless on the grass, with his arms out sideways, hands curved upwards to catch the rain.

The telephone rang.

Mrs Crask put her stew back on the stove and went to answer it.

'Oh — hullo, Daphne. Yes indeed, and how are you? *What?* You think you won't come after all? Oh — to lunch. The girls want to go to a Wimpy Bar? *I* see. But you'd like to come to tea instead? Yes. Yes, of course. No — no — not the least bit in the world.'

Slowly Mrs Crask put the receiver down. A tremendous racket of screeches and caterwauling came from the garden. Mrs Crask looked out of the kitchen window. A new tree, a well-grown young cherry, was to be seen in the middle of the front lawn. Mishkin had run up it, and was crouched in the fork, defying his pursuers.

'George!!!'

George did not answer.

'Where's that little tube?' said Mrs Crask.

When Mr Crask came home with his cigarettes, the house was quite silent. Rain fell steadily. The stew bubbled gently on top of the stove. A delicious-looking orange-flavoured apple pie stood cooling on the kitchen table.

And two new trees were growing on the front lawn.

Now You See Me, Now You Don't!

Marjorie Darke

I've got a white rosette hanging on my wall that isn't there. The rosette, I mean, not the wall! At least, it *is* there, but you can't see it. I bet you don't believe me, do you? Nobody does when I tell them. Feel the wallpaper for yourself. Go on, it's just under the horsy poster and next to my riding crop hanging on that nail. You're nearly there. A bit more to the left . . .

See!

I'll tell you about it.

The first thing you need to know is that I'm nuts about horses. You probably sussed that out already looking round my room. Posters, pony books, riding hat and boots, crop, the old bridle with the oil rag tucked in the snaffle, those bits of ribbon out of Topaz's tail. Mum says it's a tip, but I like having horsy things lying about. Makes me feel as if I've got a pony of my own. Which I haven't. Well – you can't stable a pony in a tower-block flat five floors up. There aren't any escalators and our lift is much too small. It would all be rather hopeless if it wasn't for Ellen.

Ellen's my cousin and Topaz is her pony. They live

on a farm just outside our town. I go and stay with her quite often as we are both pony freaks, so get on together like knife and fork. Aunt Win's great too, and Uncle Sidney's not bad. Dustbin's the only blot. He's Ellen's little brother. His real name is Arnold and he's six. You'll understand the nickname when I tell you that as soon as I got through the farm front door that Gymkhana Saturday morning, he ran at me asking for sweets. I gave him a pony nut, though he still had a doorstep of toast in his hand. He gobbled it and was just asking for another when Ellen came roaring up from the kitchen. Specs slipping. Hedgehog hair. She always travels like a fire engine on the way to a warehouse blaze.

'Hi, Vi!' she said. (That's me — Violet.) 'You're late. What happened?'

'Had a puncture,' I explained. 'Had to mend it.'

'Hard cheese.' Ellen had thrown off her slippers, seized a pair of old wellies and grabbed my arm, all without stopping. 'Come on, there's masses to do. The tack's okay but Topaz is a wreck.' She towed me through the kitchen, where Dustbin was polishing off the cat's milk and Aunt Win was ironing the newspaper, hardly giving me time to say 'Hi!' before we were out and crossing the yard to the stable.

Topaz *was* a wreck. Enough mud on her to fill up a fish pond. She seemed pleased to see me and began chewing my hair as soon as I got close to her. In her way she's as greedy as Dustbin.

Ellen handed me the dandy brush. 'You start that side. I'll clean her hooves.'

We slogged away, scraping and brushing, till Topaz shone like a copper kettle. Ellen stood back and admired her.

'Fantastic!'

'Super,' I agreed.

'Just needs a rub of hoof oil and she'll win the Best Kept Horse prize easy. Get the bottle for me, Vi. It's on the shelf, I think.' She had her back to me.

I rummaged amongst the junk and found a dusty bottle. Unscrewing the cap, I sniffed.

'Pooh, what a pong! Last week's kippered socks! You'll have to hold your nose.' I held it out, grinning.

Ellen turned round. Well — I've never seen anyone's face change so much. Her eyes bulged. Her cheeks went rainbow. Her mouth opened and closed like that big carp they've got in a tank at our museum. She wasn't staring at me, she had her eyes glued on the bottle. I looked too.

It hung there, twitching ever so slightly. In my fright

I almost dropped it.

There was no hand, no arm, no nothing!

'Holy cow!' I breathed, staring down. All I could see where the rest of me should have been was the dandy brush lying on the stable floor. 'Where am I?'

Ellen came close and poked at me.

'Ow!' I said. 'That nearly went in my eye.'

She let out a big breath. 'I was afraid I'd go through. You can't be a ghost, then. But what happened?'

'Dunno, do I?' I snapped. It wasn't her fault, of course, but I felt really weird and that made me cross. My skin tingled, which didn't seem right when it wasn't there. I was thinking terrible things about having to miss the Gymkhana and not being able to eat.

'Hey!' Ellen said suddenly. 'I can see your knicker elastic and your wellies.'

It was true. I was in such a flap I'd not noticed the pink circle stretched around my invisible middle, or my empty wellies. I took a step forward. The wellies moved like magic and the elastic wobbled, with the knot at the back bobbing like a cork at sea. I felt embarrassed, and wished now I'd remembered to sew it neatly when Mum told me.

Ellen had got over her first astonishment, and took the bottle off me. 'It must be this. Let's see if I'm right.'

Before I could stop her she'd tipped some oil on to a bit of old rag and was rubbing it over the dandy brush.

Nothing happened, except for smears of dirt on the rag and oil on the brush. I could see she was disappointed.

'What *exactly* did you do?' she asked.

'Sniffed it.'

For one awful moment I thought she was going to do the same, then she saw her watch. 'Crumbs, we're late. We haven't even changed yet!'

'Not much point in me changing,' I said gloomily.

'Oh, don't be daft. Even if you don't bother with anything else you'll need your riding boots and hat for the clear-round jumping.'

'How can I do clear-round jumping if I'm see-through?' I demanded.

But she wouldn't listen. 'There's no time to argue. Come on!'

I didn't budge. 'In wellies and knicker elastic . . . you have to be joking! Besides, if Aunt Win finds out what's happened she'll dose me with castor oil and tuck me up with a hot water bottle. You know how she is.'

Ellen did. 'Okay. You stay with Topaz. Shan't be long.'

She wasn't and I changed quickly. It was very odd seeing my clothes appear and disappear all the time. For some reason all the things I put on vanished – except for the elastic. I did think of leaving my knickers off, but as Ellen said – what was the point when there was elastic under my hat as well?

The Gymkhana was in a field just beyond the next village. We had to hack there. Ellen on Topaz and me on my bike. Somehow we managed to get away without Aunt Win watching, though we had a near squeak when she came dashing out of the front door after Dustbin, who had nicked a bag of crisps and an apple turnover out of the picnic basket. I'd just got hold of my bike handlegrips. They disappeared immediately, like everything that touched me. I tried not to move – tried even not to breathe, hoping my elastics would blend with the wall and the flowerbed. Luckily she didn't seem to notice. But Dustbin did. I saw his eyes go big as dinner plates. That kid could see a gnat on a chimney-pot! He didn't get a chance to say anything though, because Aunt Win swept him up and went inside.

By this time Ellen and Topaz had come out of the yard and I made her ride behind me all the way to the gate and into the lane, in case anyone happened to glance out of a window. She kept giggling, and said the bike looked so silly with bites out of it where I was sitting and everything – just like something out of a Tom and Jerry cartoon she'd seen on telly, where Tom had been blatted and turned into a ghost.

'Oh ha ha!' I said, rather sour. I mean, it isn't easy to see the funny side when it's you who's nothing but an empty space.

Ellen said: 'Don't be such a drip. Think of all the things you'll be able to do.'

I said: 'What?'

And she said: 'Go in for the competitions without paying.'

I hadn't thought of this before, but it didn't seem much of a reward. How could I compete? A horse without a rider doesn't count. I pointed this out, but all she did was go on giggling. I felt so peeved that I pedalled like mad, shooting away from her round the corner . . . and came face to space with another cyclist.

The bloke on the bike swerved and his head nearly twisted back to front as we passed. There was a squeal of brakes and a scraping thud. I glanced back and saw him sitting halfway up the grass verge, underneath his bike. He look dazed but okay, so I didn't stop, and in a minute Ellen caught up with me.

We were almost there and I was beginning to get really worried about what to do next. I'd been secretly hoping that the effect of smelling that yucky hoof oil would wear off, but so far I wasn't even cellophane thick. Another turn in the lane. Past the farm with the hayrick built like a house and . . .

There we were.

The Gymkhana was in full swing. Kids, ponies, parents, and all the people running it were seething over the field. A cotton-wool voice was blaring instructions for the next competition through a loudspeaker. I saw some ponies and riders moving towards the starting place, past an ice-cream van which stood near the hedge. The old excitement came boiling up and for a moment I forgot about being careful. Getting off my bike, I moved towards the gate where a tweedy woman was sitting at a card table collecting entrance money from the cars. She looked up, staring not at me, but at my bike upright and alone, which wheeled towards her. Very slowly she blinked twice.

And then, as her eyelids opened up for the second time, I was back. Don't ask me to tell you how it happened, because I just don't know. One minute I was see-through as windows, the next tubby and solid as Christmas pud. It was just like switching on an electric light — that fast and easy.

I don't know whether the tweedy woman actually *saw.* What I do know is that she shook her head, then pulled one of those leather brandy flasks from her pocket and emptied it into the grass.

Ellen had got off Topaz and as we went in, she murmured: 'Hard cheese!'

I knew she was still thinking about sneaking into the competitions without paying, but who cared about that? It was a pretty daft idea anyway.

The rest of the morning was great. Ellen competed in a sort of slalom, where you weave your pony in and out of some poles. She didn't win, but later she went in for the Musical Sacks and came first. Afterwards I had a go at the Egg and Spoon, but Topaz was bored or something and we were last. Then Aunt Win arrived with Dustbin and we had our picnic. All the time I stayed solid and for once didn't mind my podginess. It was so good to be able to see my knees and my feet and my sausagy hands. There was only one slight panic when we lost Dustbin. We found him in the ice-cream van 'helping' (that's his word not mine), which meant eating as much free ice-cream as he could scrounge.

The afternoon was the high spot for me. Clear-round jumping. The course was arranged in another field leading off the first, and there were seven different sorts of jumps dotted about. I ought to explain that you can have as many tries as you like until you get a clear round. Everyone who does gets a white rosette. Ellen was one of the first to enter. She flew over the first four jumps. The fifth was a natural dip in the ground made into a ditch jump with a marker pole in front and behind. Topaz stopped dead in front of this and Ellen nearly went over her head. She took her back and tried again. This time Topaz jumped easily, but of course it had spoiled the clear round. Ellen was a bit cheesed, but she had the red rosette for the Musical Sacks, so didn't feel too bad. She could have had another go straight away, but she knew how much I wanted to try and said it was only fair I should have next turn. I thought that was ace — after all, Topaz is her pony.

We let Topaz have a rest while five other people had a go. Then it was my turn.

Topaz and I get on pretty well, considering she isn't my pony and I don't get that much practice. We hadn't done too well in the Egg and Spoon, but somehow as I settled into the saddle again I had this odd feeling that everything would go just right.

I queued up and paid my 40p, watching the girl in front of me start off. Her pony knocked down two poles one after another, then missed the next jump, did three all right and finally tipped the girl into the brushwood fence.

I can do better than that, I thought, as the judge called: 'Next one!'

We were off!

The first jump was a single low pole which we took with inches to spare. Next was another slightly higher pole with a couple of oil drums underneath. Then a tree trunk. Both those we sailed over. Bales of hay followed, and that's where the trouble started. Don't get me wrong, Topaz was jumping like a dream. Hay, the ditch where she'd stopped before, a third pole with boxes in front, finally the brushwood fence — she jumped the lot without even flicking anything with her heels. No . . . it was *me!* As we took off before the hay bales, I vanished! Where I held the reins, where I sat on the saddle, where I touched Topaz with my legs — all that had vanished as well. The poor thing was as full of holes as a paper doily. By the time we touched down I was back. But I disappeared as we jumped the ditch. Again I came back, only to disappear for a third time. It was like being one of those Christmas fairy lights popping on and off every second. I felt dizzy, but there was nothing I could do except hang on and try remembering everything I'd learned about how to help your pony jump properly. I was too busy to see if the judges had noticed anything.

Of course they had!

As Topaz and I (see-through) came over the brushwood fence and landed (solid), the judge at the exit was as white as the rosette in her hand. I knew we'd had a clear round, so I rode up to collect it.

She backed away. Eyes like organ stops. Then she coughed and gasped: 'Wait a minute!'

I waited.

The other judges came hurrying up, and as the exit judge joined them I could hear them arguing:

' . . . clear round. Yes, it was. Definitely.'

'But over four of the jumps the pony had no rider. That can't mean a clear round.'

'She couldn't have fallen off and remounted, surely?'

'She came over that last fence and *appeared,* I tell you. There's nothing in the rules to cover *that!*'

'But I was on Topaz all the time. Really I was,' I burst out, unable to bear it any longer. It would be too mean if they refused to give Topaz and me the rosette we'd earned. 'I only went see-through for a second. It happens sometimes.'

Then an old bloke in a Sherlock Holmes hat, who seemed to be chief judge, said: 'No, there is certainly no rule to cover instant vanishing, but I think no one can say it wasn't a *clear* round. You have won your rosette!' and he burst into a roar of laughter.

Then came the oddest thing of all. He insisted on tying the rosette round my sleeve, and as he did, it *vanished!* It was there all right. I could feel it. So could

Ellen and Aunt Win when they tried. But it's never come back. Not from that day to this. Well — you know, don't you? You felt it. Sometimes I wonder if it did, whether I might vanish again. It hasn't happened so far and I get goose pimples when I think that way.

And my wellies and elastics staying solid all the time? Funny you should ask about that. I don't know the answer really. They were all rubbery things, of course. Dustbin thought of that. He's not a blot *all* the time. Sometimes he can be quite clever.

Ellen and I are still nuts about horses. We go to Gymkhanas too. But we never use hoof oil. To tell the truth we've never been able to find the bottle again. We have a sneaky feeling Dustbin knows something about that too, though he won't ever let on. But several of the farm cats have a funny way of just being there all of a sudden . . . and vanishing just as quick!

Nurse Matilda Goes to the Hairdresser's

Christianna Brand

Once upon a time there was a huge family of children and they were terribly, terribly naughty.

There was so many of these children that I can't even tell you all their names – even their parents had to divide them into the Big Ones and the Middling Ones and the Little Ones. The littlest was the Baby. The Baby was really a splendid character; it had fat bent legs and its nappies were always falling down round its fat pink knees, but it kept up with the other children to the last ounce of its strength. It talked a curious language all of its own.

Their mother and father were called Mr and Mrs Brown; and when their children got really unbearably naughty, they had fallen into the habit of sending for Nurse Matilda.

Nurse Matilda was a rather special kind of nurse. She was terribly ugly – the ugliest person you ever saw in your life. Her hair was scraped back into a bun, sticking straight out at the back of her head like a teapot handle; and her face was very round and wrinkly and she had two little black boot-button eyes, and her nose! – she had a nose like two potatoes. She wore a rusty black dress and a rusty black bonnet all covered with trembly black jet, and in one hand she carried a very big black stick. What Nurse Matilda could do when she banged on the floor with that big black stick!

One day, Nurse Matilda said to the children, 'I am going out for a couple of hours. You had better have a little sleep till I get back. That will keep you nice and quiet.'

'Oh, no!' cried the children, 'we don't want to have a little sleep!' and, 'Oh, no!' cried the Baby. 'Not wonky giggy keep!' But Nurse Matilda just banged gently on the floor with her stick and all of a sudden there they were, curled up on sofas and chairs like drowsy little bees, snoring drowsy little bee-snores. Nurse Matilda smiled round upon them — and when she smiled, she didn't look nearly so ugly after all — and went away.

On the stairs she passed by Mrs Brown. 'I think the children will be nice and quiet,' she said.

Mrs Brown was very sweet but she really was rather foolish and she could never believe that her darling children were naughty at all; so she went on up and said, 'Wake up, children. I'm taking you all to the hairdresser's.'

'Oh, no!' cried the children. 'We don't want to go to the hairdresser's!' and, 'Nock wonky go!' cried the Baby. But Mrs Brown took no notice. She was sure they would really love going to the hairdresser's and, as it turned out, she was perfectly right.

Mrs Brown's hairdressers were very grand and their salon was very grand too, full of shelves and mirrors and plush chairs for sitting in under the hair-driers, and lots and lots of pots and bottles and sprays and hairpins and little bottles of sticky enamel for painting the ladies' nails. The children looked round with a gleam in their eyes and, to their great joy, saw that among all the ladies sitting round having their hair done was a very stout horrid little girl they knew, called Evangeline, with her poor thin chilblainy governess, Miss Prawn, and her horrid little pug-dog, which with great originality was called Pug. Outside the door, in her bath-chair, sat Miss Prawn's horrid old mother, nibbling on a cake of soap. She had a quite inordinate passion for soap.

The salon was run by two Russian gentlemen – at least, I think they must have been Russian because their names were Mr Cuttalotovit and Mr Choppitorlorf. They simply hated being hairdressers and wished like anything that ladies had been bald and wouldn't have to have their hair shampooed and set and curled and done up on top of their heads. They did not care for children at all and looked very gloomy when Mrs Brown came in with her family all filing in behind her, the Baby as usual trotting gamely along at the end with its nappies just about to fall down.

'You had better commink into der chompooink room ant havink your hair shampoot,' they said to Mrs Brown, hoping in their hearts that when she took off her hat, they'd find that she hadn't got any.

But Mrs Brown had lots of lovely long hair and she was away for quite a good while in the shampooing room.

I'm afraid now I'll have to tell you what was happening when she got back.

The children had discovered the nail varnish and were sharing it round among themselves; it turned out to be simply splendid stuff, as good as glue.

David had got a large bottle of shampoo and poured it into an upturned hair-dryer, and Tora had switched on the dryer and now all the air was filling with snowflakes of lather. Daniel had smeared nail varnish on Mr Choppitorlorf's shoes and now he was glued together from the ankles down and, to his amazement, could only progress in a series of curious hops. Alexandra had poured lots of it into a chair and sat stout Evangeline firmly down in it, and Isabelle had painted pink blotches of it all over the mirrors. Emma had caught the sound of Miss Prawn's mother in her bathchair, baying for more soap, and slipped out and handed her a bottle of shampoo, which seemed to do just as well. Marina had discovered some stuff for removing unwanted hair and sprayed it all over Mr Cuttalotovit's dinky little golden beard. Augusta was assuring poor Miss Prawn that the Hedgehog Haircut was just the thing for her, and was sticking hundreds of hairpins all over her head till she looked like Mrs Tiggywinkle; and Ginevra was slapping a mud-pack all over the face of a lady called Miss Pickelstick – who, in fact, had only popped her head in at the door to say that there was an old person in a bathchair outside, hardly visible through a foam of bubbles and should something be done about it? Louisa, finding stout Evangeline stuck in her chair and unable to struggle, was dyeing her hair a lovely emerald green. Charlotte was lathering Pug with lots of fluffy shampoo and now he thought he was a white poodle and would be called Pooch which would be even worse than Pug; and Horace had found the cloakroom and was smearing the inside of the ladies' hats with a nice, greasy face cream. Edward had collected a lot of umbrellas and was handing them round to the ladies, who were stumbling about in the snowstorm – for the lather had whipped up splendidly and now the whole salon was filled with it. They were stumbling because Simon had sprayed sticky hair-setting stuff all over the floor, except where Matthew had smeared in some brilliantine.

All the other children had been doing simply dreadful things too.

Mrs Brown came through from the shampooing room and stopped short. 'Oh, dear!' she said. 'Whatever can be happening?' That her dear children should be in any way involved, never entered her head.

'Smolenskayavushka!' cried Mr Choppitorlorf, hopping in after her like an outraged kangaroo. 'Moscovitoshka! Leningradnishanka!' (You see — I told you he must be Russian!)

Mr Cuttalotovit said nothing. He was speechlessly snatching at small yellow tufts which seemed to be detaching themselves from his little golden beard.

The air by now was really quite thick with its snowstorm of lather and through it could be discerned the darting figures of the children and the large and terrified figures of the ladies, umbrellas up, crashing into one another as they blundered and slipped on the greasy patches or (brought up short by the hair-spray) stood rooted to the floor, umbrellas locked together like the antlers of fighting stags.

'Oh, *dear!*' said Mrs Brown.

Such ladies as had found their way to the cloakroom were now in a terrible taking, blinded by their hats, which, thanks to the grease, had slid down over their eyes and ears and blinded and deafened them. Joanna had slipped a blue hairnet over the head of a simply huge singer called Madame Cabbargio who, to her horror, found she could not open her mouth and was in deadly fear that she might never sing again; nor could she understand why suddenly her enormous round face should be covered with an alarming criss-cross of bright blue lines. 'M'f, m'f, m'f!' cried poor Madame Cabbargio; and from outside came other muffled cries of 'M'f, m'f, *m'f!*' Miss Prawn's old mother had gone too far with the shampoo.

'To the rescue!' cried kind Miss Pickelstick, flinging open the salon door and clutching wildly through the

bubbles at Miss Prawn's old mother's bathchair. From afar came the loud clanging of bells as ambulances, rescue teams and fire-engines bore down upon the scene. A small crowd had gathered but, at the sight of Miss Pickelstick's face covered in its mud-pack, they fell back and released their hold upon the bathchair. Slowly the balloon of irridescent bubbles began to rise into the air. 'Ow! Ow!' cried Miss Pickelstick. 'Ow! Ow!' cried all the spectators. 'Ow! Ow! *Ow!*' cried Miss Prawn's mother faintly from inside her massed bubbles, licking shampoo off her chin and blowing it out again. By now she was chimney high.

Inside the salon, the opening of the door had released a little of the snowstorm, and such ladies as were not blinded by umbrellas or greasy hats, caught sight of their faces in the mirrors and saw that they appeared to be covered with large pink blotches. 'The plague!' cried the most alarmist among them. 'Frostbite!' cried the rest, shivering in the dank, lather-filled air. But, of course, when they turned away from the enamel-spotted mirrors there was nothing to see. 'What are *you* complaining about?' they said to each other indignantly. 'There's nothing wrong with *you.* Just look at *me!*' '*You're* all right,' said the others. '*I'm* covered in blotches.' 'No, you're not,' said the first ones. 'Yes, I am,' said the other ones, all getting crosser and crosser. They turned upon Madame Cabbargio, sitting rooted in her chair, soundless, and covered with her net-work of blue. 'Aren't I?' they cried. 'Isn't she?' they cried. 'You decide for us,' they all demanded with one voice.

'I harnt,' mumbled Madame Cabbargio, sitting gloomily munching hair-net. 'I harnt halk.' Or sing! Would she never be able to sing again? Long ago, the children had translated for her an Italian song which she was practising for a party being given by their fearsome great-aunt, Great-Aunt Adelaide Stitch. 'La Great-Aunt Adelaide-a ees a seely old fool-a,' Madame Cabbargio had innocently warbled. Aunt Adelaide, being stone-deaf, had observed the tumultuous applause of the audience and been perfectly delighted, and so, of course, had Madame Cabbargio. She nowadays adapted the song to the name of whatever hostess she was singing for and, as long as they happened to be deaf, enjoyed enormous success. Was all this now to be lost? She made one tremendous effort to reply to the ladies, the net split from side to side, and she was free!

'Eesa narteeng wrong veet you,' she shouted angrily, belting it out with the sudden release of her jaws, 'but vaart abouts me? Suppose never more I am seenging so beautiful?' And to make quite certain, she threw back her head and burst into an extremely loud aria. 'Your tiny hent is frooooozen!' howled Madame Cabbargio.

The ladies held up their hands with small squeals of horror, looking for more blotches, and Pug, always much moved by music, lifted up his lather-covered muzzle and shrilly joined in. 'Wow-wow-woooooooow!' hooted Pug, and Evangeline, fixed in her chair and staring electrified at the emerald green pigtails looming at her through the floating lather, joined in on a note hardly to be distinguished from Pug's. The whole world seemed filled with lather and howling and the clash of umbrellas.

'Oh, *dear!*' said Mrs Brown. I simply will not repeat to you what Mr Choppitorlorf was saying. Mr Cuttalotovit quietly mourned his departed beard.

Outside, things were going — well, curiously. An extension ladder had been run up after Miss Prawn's old mother as she floated in her cocoon of bubbles, sucking in more and more shampoo. She was at the bottle again — it was her only comfort — and every time she cried out 'Ow! Ow!', which she did all the time, she blew out more

bubbles, so that as fast as the balancing fireman grasped at any bit of her clothing that poked out through the delicate casing of her balloon, the bubbles blew up again into their rainbow cloud and off she floated, further and further out of reach. 'Ow! Ow!' cried Miss Prawn's old mother, growing more and more alarmed, and 'Ow dang!' cried the brave fireman, swaying about at the top of his ladder, clutching at nothingness.

Miss Prawn emerged from the salon, complete with new hair-do, and stood gazing upward in dismay. Her mother was a simply horrid old lady really and Miss Prawn should have been devoutly praying that she would float right up to heaven, where she by no means deserved to go, but instead she too cried out, 'Ow! Ow!', and wrung her poor, chilblainy hands. 'Let me go to her, let me go to her!' cried Miss Prawn. 'I will reason with her about her intake of shampoo!'

'You do that,' cried the fireman from the top of the ladder, thankfully climbing down.

Miss Prawn clasped her chilblains about the lower rung of the ladder and, assisted by the fireman and the now enormous crowd, all scurrying about her like a nest of ants propelling a thin piece of twig, she was pushed and harried on up the ladder till she came to the top. 'Come back, come back!' bleated Miss Prawn, dangerously swaying, after her ballooning mama.

'M'f, m'f!' cried her mother, much muffled by surrounding bubbles.

'Yes, you can,' cried Miss Prawn. 'Keep your mouth closed and don't suck in any more shampoo!'

'M'f, m'f, *m'f* it,' said the old lady rebelliously.

'Yes, I know you like it, but it's getting you nowhere,' pleaded Miss Prawn. In fact this was not strictly true: it *was* getting the old lady somewhere, and fast, for there was a church spire quite near by and sooner or later the bathchair with its frail veil of bubbles was going to cannon into it with an almighty bonk.

'Stick out your hands,' implored Miss Prawn, 'and try to paddle your way back.' And she told the one and only fib of her kind and virtuous life. 'I've got a nice big bar of kitchen soap for you here,' she said.

Miss Prawn said this in the nick of time, for the bottle of shampoo was coming to an end and soon the bubbles would all pop away and the bathchair would be left sailing through the air unsupported, which is not a thing that bathchairs can keep up for very long. Miss Prawn's mother decided for the bar of soap, thrust out stick-like arms and began to paddle with her hands through the air, like oars. Slowly, the great, softly radiant balloon began to turn and move back towards the top of the ladder where Miss Prawn, with outflung hands, clung perilously, all ready to grasp it.

But you can't stand all that long at the top of a swaying fireman's ladder with your arms outstretched. Miss Prawn began to wobble and clutched wildly at the top rung; and at that moment the balloon floated gently over and settled down upon the new hedgehog hair.

And phttt, phttt, phttt! went the bubbles, punctured by hair-pins right, left and centre, and 'Ow! Ow! Ow!' cried Miss Prawn and Miss Prawn's mother with one voice.

Below, in the packed street, the noise was deafening. Madame Cabbargio with her blue checkered face was still loudly giving voice as to the condition of the frost-bitten hands, Pug howling loyally in unison;

Evangeline was humping herself along with out-thrust bottom still glued to the seat of her chair, boo-hoo-hooing quite dreadfully at the plight of her dear Prawnie at the end of a long ladder with her old mother in a bathchair apparently sitting on the top of her prickly head. Mr Choppitorlorf was uttering Russian oaths of increasingly awful significance, and Mr Cuttalotovit was baying with despair as the last of the tufts blew away from his chin, leaving it naked to the air. The umbrella ladies were still meeting, heads down, with a clashing of metal ribs and rending of silk, while the greasy-hat ladies were still barging blindly about, banging at all and sundry with their handbags and loudly demanding release. Now and again, one of those still left in the salon would finally wrench her feet from the restraining glue on the floor and come glissading out into the crowd on a patch of grease.

'Oh dear, oh dear!' said Mrs Brown. A tiny touch of the truth was beginning to dawn and she gazed up at the dissolving bubble in positive alarm.

The children also gazed up in alarm. 'Oh, goodness!' they said. It was no longer funny — what was happening up there.

'Go goognick!' said the Baby. But the Baby was gazing *down.* Its nappies had fallen right off and were forming a little figure of eight round its fat pink feet.

And suddenly . . .

Suddenly down the street came stumping a small black figure, in a rusty black dress with a rusty black bonnet all trembly with jet, and a wrinkly round face and two little boot-button eyes, and a nose — a nose like two potatoes. And in one hand she carried a very big black stick. And the children all cried out: 'It's Nurse Matilda!'

'Ick Nurk Magiggy!' cried the Baby, the only one to say it joyfully.

Nurse Matilda looked around her at the packed

crowd gazing upwards, and she glanced upwards and she looked back at the children, all standing with their hands clapped over their mouths staring back at her with scared round eyes. And she banged once on the pavement with her big black stick.

And — I don't know how it happened, but the children found that they were right back doing what they had been doing just one hour ago: filing quietly into the hairdressing salon after Mrs Brown, the Baby stumping along in the rear with its nappies back in their usual place, in other words, just about to fall down. And there was no crowd in the street any more and no sign of Miss Prawn up any ladder — well, there wasn't any ladder, so she couldn't be — and no sign of her horrid old mother eating soap in her bathchair and no sign of emerald green Evangeline and no pug; not even any ladies butting into one another with their umbrellas, their hats rammed down over their eyes. And no splodges on the looking-glasses and no grease nor any sticky-stuff on the floor. And Mr Choppitorlorf was talking English again and Mr Cuttalotovit was complete with his little golden beard. Nurse Matilda had banged with that big black stick and everything was back, just as it had been. Except . . .

Except that Mrs Brown was not asking to have her own hair done but was looking round upon her children and saying, 'I should like to have their hair cut, please,' and the children were meekly finding chairs and settling into them. Only the Baby lifted big wondering blue eyes and put its fat hands over its curls and said, 'Nock cuck *my* hair?'

Mr Choppitorlorf and Mr Cuttalotovit were beside themselves with joy at finding so many heads of hair to be cut. 'A lot off?' they said to Mrs Brown, reaching out for huge scissors and opening and shutting them like the jaws of two crocodiles.

'*All* off,' said Mrs Brown.

All off! Snip, snip, snip went the scissors, and whhisssssh, whhisssssh, whhisssssh, went the children's hair, falling softly to the floor. Soon all the Big Ones were finished. The Middling Ones looked at them with unutterable horror. 'They're bald!' they said.

'Yes,' said Mr Cuttalotovit and Mr Choppitorlorf, and with gleaming eyes they turned their attention to the Middling Ones.

'Nock wanka ge gald,' said the Baby, its hands on its head.

Mr Cuttalotovit and Mr Choppitorlorf paid no attention but set about the Middling Ones. 'Bald?' they said to Mrs Brown, snapping the crocodile scissors with eager hands. 'Bald,' said Mrs Brown. 'As eggs,' she added, smiling affectionately, as though her dear children would simply love to be as bald as eggs. And snip, snip, snip went the terrible scissors at the heads of the Middling Ones.

And the Little Ones. 'If we rub some stuff over their heads,' said Mr Choppitorlorf, delighted at the thought of so many people who would never have to come to him to have their hair done, 'it will never grow again.'

'Oh?' said Mrs Brown, beginning to look a little doubtful.

'Think of the saving,' said Mr Cuttalotovit, 'in brushes and combs' (and with so many children, it certainly would be considerable) 'and shampoo — '

'And,' said Mr Choppitorlorf joyfully, 'coming again to have it cut.'

But the look of doubt had given the children a gleam of hope. 'Oh, please,' they cried, 'don't let them rub stuff on us to make our hair never grow again! Please don't!'

Nurse Matilda stood four-square in the middle of the

salon, watching it all with her little black boot-button eyes. 'Nurse Matilda,' said Mrs Brown, 'what do *you* think?'

'I think that the children have been exceedingly naughty,' said Nurse Matilda. 'But more than that, I think they have been unkind. They have greatly upset these two gentlemen — ' she looked rather fixedly at the little golden beard '— and distressed a great many harmless ladies by making them think they had frostbite or the plague, not to mention blue criss-crosses all over the face; and frightened others by blinding them with slipping-down hats and bangings of umbrellas and sticking and sliding on the floor. They have scared another child, however stout and unlovable, by glueing her to her chair and giving her green hair, and made a helpless pug believe himself to be a poodle, which he had no wish to be; and they have terrified a poor lady already suffering quite enough with her chilblains and her horrid old mother, by having the old lady carried away over the roof-tops in a foam of bubbles and nearly bonking into a church spire. The fact that a large crowd of onlookers loved every minute of it,' added Nurse Matilda, 'has nothing to do with it. From first to last, the children have been most thoughtless and unkind and caused suffering; so let them suffer in their turn.'

'But bald?' cried the children. 'For the rest of our lives? We don't want to be bald.'

'Nock wanky ge gald!' cried the poor baby, still guarding its head with pink, outspread, starfish hands; and great tears gathered in its big blue eyes.

But Mr Cuttalotovit and Mr Choppitorlorf took no notice at all but lifted it up and dumped it into a chair much too big for it, and tucked a towel round its neck; and snip! went the scissors, and a golden curl fell and lay, silky and shining, on the floor.

'Stop, stop!' cried the children. 'Don't cut the Baby's hair! All right, rub our heads with the stuff to make us all bald for the rest of our lives – but don't cut the Baby's hair! It doesn't want its hair cut, it doesn't want to be bald. Please don't cut it – we'd rather be bald ourselves!'

'For the rest of your lives?' said Nurse Matilda.

'Yes, yes!' cried the children. 'We've been naughty, we've been horrid and unkind and we've got to be punished. But the Baby's done nothing, don't cut the Baby's hair!'

'Ah,' said Nurse Matilda. 'That's better, isn't it? That at least is kind.' And she lifted the Baby up from the too-big chair and held it close on her rusty black shoulder with its soft, tear-wet cheek against her own. They all stood round her with their poor bald heads like a huge clutch of pink eggs. 'Sometimes,' she said to Mrs Brown, 'what amuses us is rude and hurtful to others. But I think that so much true self-sacrifice on this occasion might put that right?' And she banged, but this time quite softly, on the salon floor.

And – how it could happen, once again I simply don't know – suddenly with a great deal of stretching and yawning, the children found themselves waking up from a deep sleep, curled on sofas and chairs in the dear old nursery at home; and Nurse Matilda was standing in the doorway with Mrs Brown. 'I knew they would be good while I was out,' she said, 'if they all had a nice little sleep.' And she smiled at them. 'Have you had pleasant dreams?' she said.

And, do you know – it was a curious thing – but, just for a moment, when Nurse Matilda smiled, she didn't look ugly at all.

A Fishy Tale or, How I Joined the Mixed Maggots and Bottom Feeders Told to Gene Kemp

John Sweet

My Dad says the best thing to do is to forget all about it. Especially as I lost my wellingtons. I suppose he's right, really, but since you asked about it, here goes, Mzz Kemp.

I was getting tired, I reckon, and my concentration slipped and so did I, into the canal, at the edge where all the tall plants and reeds line the bank, deep and green and mysterious, full of insects and weird crawlies. And there in the middle of the canal is the deep channel where all the fish swim along. Yes, I love fishing. I like going fishing with my Dad better than anything else. Better even than football, I think . . . All them fish, browny red dace, roach with orange fins, spotted perch, all spiky, you need a rag to protect your hands when you get him off the hook, and down at the bottom of the centre channel there's the spotted brown gudgeon, a bottom feeder, and the stone loach with stick-out lips, like this, whuwh, see?

Of course, you do get the nobs putting in a grand appearance sometimes, the salmon and the silver brown trout, but not for me with my licence at £1.50. If you do nabble one, you put it back quick.

Oh, it's a fantastic sport.

And the sport isn't just to catch the fish, but to land it, easy, easy. If you wind in too quickly the line will break, because of the friction, so you must do it slowly to let it move around in angles which tires the fish, and it's easier to pull out smoothly. Don't let the line go loose or the fish jumps, the hook slides and the fish escapes.

You need the feel, like.

This Sunday I'm telling you about, my Dad took me out about four. It was a smashing day, hot for October,

with brown and yellow leaves lying in heaps to shuffle your feet through, scrunch, scrunch. I was glad to go, not only because, as I've told you, I like going fishing with my Dad better than anything, but because it had been that sort of a Sunday. My elder brother was out of the house somewhere, but the rest were hanging about all over the place, shouting and bossing me about, that's the worst of having four sisters, and you know what our Sandra is like, Mzz Kemp. Our house isn't very big neither, and my Mum made me do jobs, but it didn't really matter, not inside, because I knew I was going fishing with my Dad.

We set off, and it was still warm and sunny, though the mist was beginning to stir in little smoky spirals as we walked down the long hill that goes to the river and beyond to the canal. It's called Fore Street, and our teacher, you, Mzz Kemp, told us the Romans marched down there, long ago, and people before that, and it's a pretty steep hill, though that didn't bother me, *then*.

At last we reached the canal, and there's a road on one side for cars, and a path on the other for people and dogs, but half-way to Double Locks is a bridge, a really narrow bridge, and there the road crosses over becoming a path and the path becomes the road on the other side, bit daft really, not that it bothered me and Dad, because we were walking anyway, but it is tricky to drive across. Two posts stop cars trying to drive on to the path. Just beyond the bridge, where it's fine for fishing with the banks all green and quiet and beautiful, I sat down with my tackle and Dad wandered on a bit. I put down my bag for the fish and my rag to handle them with, then I made sure the eyes were level, pulled the lines up through them, fixed the little round band, the float and the hook, judged the weights, put them on, stood up straight and cast without maggots. Then I got the maggots on to the hook, pushing them with my thumb, and cast. My landing net was ready and the float was okay. The red bit goes under when you've got a bite.

Only I hadn't. And I didn't. I waited and I waited and I waited.

The sun painted the sky, pink and purple and orange and red, while I sat there on my little folding

stool, waiting. No bite at all. Not a sausage. Not a dicky bird. Not a dicky bird of a sausage. Not a nibble.

I could feel a nibble inside, though.

I was hungry. I was very hungry. I was starving.

Roast pork with apple sauce and crackling when we got home, Mum had said. I thought about roast pork and apple sauce and crackling. I pictured it on my plate. I pictured me eating it. I felt even hungrier.

The sun pushed off to the other side of the world or wherever it goes, taking all the colour with it. Grey mist trailed everywhere. My fingers grew cold and stiff. Dad came along and asked how I was doing, no good I said, him neither, we'd pack it in soon and go home.

'Another minute, Dad,' I asked, as he turned away. I didn't want to return with no catch and Sandra laughing like a drain, and I don't know why, but at the very thought of Sandra, my chair slipped, so did I, and there I was, slip, sliding away on my back into the reeds, and down, down, down into the water, coming up over my wellies, colder than cold, shock, horror. Somehow I turned, grabbed a rough and unkind sort of plant and yelled for Dad, who had gone some way away.

And a car came over the bridge, a man's head stuck out of the window, yelling, 'Look at that little kid. He's gonna drown! Stop!'

It didn't stop. It came roaring on. Towards me. My cold hands were slipping. Any minute now, I'd be among the fish I'd been after, earlier, and I didn't fancy the idea much. I didn't want to meet the bottom feeders on their own level. I didn't think we'd have much to say to each other down there amongst all that cold mud. 'Dad!' I yelled even louder. I couldn't see him, and I was slipping further all the time.

But if I couldn't see Dad, I could see the car. It was heading straight towards me and it didn't look as if it knew how to stop. It seemed as if I had a choice. Either be run over or drowned. I thought fast, very fast. And there was only one way to go so I went. Backwards into the canal. Right up to my neck in cold slimy canal water, me and my maggots, line tackle and all, sinking right down into what seemed enough mud to submerge a submarine. I thought I could hear the fishes laughing all the way to Double Locks.

The car swerved, hitting the posts, one went into the water, just missing me, the other stayed put and the car rose up on it. The back door flew open and out jumped a man.

'Don't worry, son. I'm here.'

He certainly was. Water splashed everywhere, as if some huge whale was spouting off. He grabbed me by the neck and headed for the bank.

'I'm all right. I can swim,' I shouted, but he wasn't listening. Holding me like he was a dog with his favourite bone, he stumbled on, then fell forward, me with him.

'I can't swim,' he shouted, dropping me, and waving his arms about.

'I'm coming,' shouted another man, leaping towards us. I managed to move just in time. This splash was more like a freak tidal wave. Nowhere was left untouched. But I'd seen Dad on the bank and I was getting to him fast.

'It's all right,' shouted my Dad. 'Don't all go in!'

Too late. Another flying body hit the water, now full of bodies and one post. The canal was having a busy evening. Together we arrived at the bank where Dad pulled us out one by one. A lot of panting and spitting and coughing went on. That canal water doesn't taste nice at all.

'We saved your boy,' said one.

'Yeah,' said my Dad.

'Aren't you gonna thank us?'

'Well, thank you, yes, and I hope you enjoyed your bit of fun in there, but I feel I must say that first of all, he's the school swimming champion, and next, you couldn't drown a rabbit in there, let alone three big blokes like you. John, where's your wellingtons?'

'In the mud, Dad. They came off.'

'Well, we'd better get walking then, before you catch cold. It's a fair step.'

The driver had righted the car by now. The others climbed in dripping wet.

'We can't offer you a lift,' one said.

'Funny you not being able to swim, Reg. I never knew that,' I heard one of them say. Reg made a sort of angry roaring noise as the car drove off.

It was a long way home. Especially in wet-socked feet. And I thought I'd got a fish down my back, but it turned out to be a slimy weed. I kept thinking of them Roman soldiers as we walked back up that hill, Mzz Kemp, and how they had to keep going when they didn't feel like it. Once a dog came out and barked at us, but he soon stopped when my Dad said a few words to him. But it was a long way home.

Roast pork and apple sauce and crackling's scrumptious when you eat it in front of a hot fire after a bath. Even Sandra was nice to me. She didn't laugh. Much.

Guess what I'm doing next Sunday?

Going fishing, of course.

Auntie Bea's Day Out
Diana Wynne Jones

'I shall take the children for a lovely day at the seaside tomorrow,' said Auntie Bea.

The children felt miserable. Auntie Bea was huge, with a loud voice. She had been staying with the Pearsons for a week then, and they all felt crushed and cross.

'You needn't bother to drive us, Tom,' said Auntie Bea. 'I can easily go by bus.' This was Auntie Bea's way of telling Mr Pearson he was to drive them to the seaside.

Mr Pearson looked very cheerful. 'Isn't that lucky? I have to take the car for its MOT tomorrow.'

When Auntie Bea decided to do something, she did it. She turned to Mrs Pearson. 'Well, you can help me carry the things, Eileen.'

Mrs Pearson hastily discovered that she was going to the dentist.

'Then Nancy will help,' said Auntie Bea. 'Nancy's so sensible.'

'No, I'm not,' said Nancy.

'So that's all right,' said Auntie Bea. She never attended to anything the children said. 'Nancy can look after Debbie, and Simon can carry the things.'

The number of things Auntie Bea needed for a day at the seaside would have been about right if she was going to climb Mount Everest. Mr Pearson helped her pile them in the hall, in twenty-two separate heaps. Auntie Bea was so afraid of losing or forgetting some of them that she wrote out twenty-two labels, each with their names and address on it, and tied them to the bundles. Meanwhile, Mrs Pearson cut up four loaves to make the number of sandwiches Auntie Bea thought they would need.

'And little jellies in yoghurt cups,' Auntie Bea said, racing into the kitchen. '*Such* a good idea!'

Mrs Pearson was so glad to be getting rid of Auntie Bea for a day that she made them two jellies each.

'I feel like a human sacrifice,' Simon said. 'How does she think I can carry all that and manage Honey as well?' Honey was due to have puppies any day now. Simon was too anxious about her to leave her behind.

Auntie Bea came downstairs shaking out a vast swimsuit. It was electric blue with shiny orange hearts all over it. Nancy blinked, and wondered what Auntie Bea would look like wearing it.

'That's pretty,' said Debbie, who loved bright colours. 'I shall make Teddy a swimsuit like that.'

'I hope it rains,' said Nancy.

Unfortunately, the next day was bright and sunny. But they missed the early bus, because of Teddy and Honey. Debbie had pinned a scarf round Teddy like a nappy, and she had written him a label too. *Deb's Ted wiv care in Emurjunsy fone Millwich 29722.*

As soon as Auntie Bea saw Teddy, she said, 'No, dear. We only take things we need today.'

Debbie's face took on its most mulish look, and the argument only ended when Auntie Bea saw Honey drooping joylessly on the end of her lead.

'You can't take him, dear. He might have his puppies at any moment!' Just as Auntie Bea never attended to children, she never attended to whether dogs were shes.

That argument was only finished when Simon found he could not carry all his bundles, even without Honey.

'You'll have to leave the stove and the kettle,' said Mrs Pearson, very anxious to see them off.

'In that case, we must take plenty of boiled water!' said Auntie Bea. 'Think of the germs!'

So Simon's bundles were repacked and they set off to catch the later bus. Nancy went first with a light load of: one tartan rug, one carrier-bag of sandwiches, a first aid box and a bundle of buckets and spades. Auntie Bea sailed behind hung about with: one folding chair, one striped umbrella, three pints of milk, a bag of sweaters, a bag of suntan cream, a packet of sandwiches, two dozen hard-boiled eggs, a complete change of Outsize clothes, three books and a radio. Debbie trotted behind that with: a bundle of towels, a beachball in a string bag and a basket full of jellies and cake, with Teddy defiantly sitting in it too. A long, long way behind came Simon. He was not sure what was in the rucksack, nor what was in his other six bundles, but he could see thermos flasks sticking out of one and an electric torch out of another. His knees buckled under it all, and Honey kept tangling her lead round them. Honey did not seem happy.

'It will serve him right if he has his puppies in the sea,' Auntie Bea said, and counted all the bundles to make sure they had remembered them all.

Nothing much happened on the bus ride, except that Honey threatened to be sick. When they got to Millhaven, it was quite late in the morning and already very crowded.

'Crowds, germs!' said Auntie Bea, counting everything again. 'We should have caught the early bus.' She hoisted up her twelve bundles and set off happily down the steps to the sand, calling, 'Don't bother to help with all this. I can manage perfectly.'

They struggled after her down the steps and caught her up on the sand.

'Debbie,' said Auntie Bea, 'you take the umbrella. If Nancy takes the folding chair, I can manage perfectly.'

'No, I won't,' said Debbie. 'It was you brought it.'

'Why don't we stop just here?' Nancy asked.

Debbie's refusal brought out the worst in Auntie Bea. She gave a scornful look round the deckchairs, rugs and sandcastles on the crowded beach, and called out to the man who hired the deckchairs in her loudest, most hooting voice: 'My good man, can you direct me to somewhere less crowded?'

The deckchair man scratched his head. 'Well, it thins out a bit up there, ma'am, but you can't go in the rocks. Tourists are not allowed on the island.'

Auntie Bea stuck up her head indignantly at being called a tourist and set off at a trot where the man pointed, hooting to the children to come along. They ploughed after her, making zig-zags round the other families, who all stared, because Auntie Bea kept turning round and hooting at them. To the right were the lovely white waves of the sea, rolling, folding and breaking with a joyful smash, but Auntie Bea would not hear of stopping. Honey, on the other hand, would not walk. She had never seen the sea before. All she knew was that it was the biggest bath in the universe, and she dreaded baths. Simon had a terrible time with her.

Nancy suggested that they stopped for the donkeys, and for the swings, and for one of the ice-cream carts. But Auntie Bea just cried out 'Germs!' and scudded on.

She would not stop until they had left all the people behind, and there was nothing but rocks. There was a kind of road of rocks stretching into the sea and, at the end of the road, an island. It was quite small – only big enough to hold a tuft of trees.

'The very place!' cried Auntie Bea, and went out over the rocks like Steve Ovett winning a race.

Honey, for some reason, was even more afraid of the island than the sea. Simon had to walk backwards, dragging her. When he turned round at the end, he found there was a barbed-wire fence round the island and a large notice on the gate: ISLAND ISLAND KEEP OUT.

There was no time to wonder about that. Auntie Bea was already charging through the trees. Simon dragged

Honey past another notice: NO TRESPASSERS, and yet another: TRESPASSERS WILL BE SORRY. By that time, Auntie Bea had stopped and he caught up.

'I don't think we ought to be on this island,' Nancy was saying.

'Nobody's afraid of three ignorant notices, dear,' said Auntie Bea. 'We're going to camp here.'

Everyone was too tired to protest. They threw down the bundles and thankfully tipped the sand out of their shoes. Honey lay down, panting. She looked rather ill. Auntie Bea prepared to put on her swimsuit. First she spread the rug out. Then she arranged the chair and the screen and the umbrella to make a sort of hut. Finally, she crawled mountainously in to undress.

Nancy and Debbie undressed where they were, and

Simon tried to do the same. His shirt was stuck to his back by something sticky and smelling loudly of strawberry.

'I think the jellies have leaked on you,' Debbie said, and crawled over to look at the yoghurt cups in her basket. The sun had melted every one, and, in the mysterious way things happen at the seaside, every one was half full of sand. Teddy was soaked in stawberry juice. 'This is *awful!*' said Debbie, and put Teddy on the branch of a tree to dry.

'Don't grumble, dear,' Auntie Bea called out of her hut. 'We're having a *lovely* time!'

The island gave a curious shudder. It made them very uneasy.

'Auntie Bea,' said Nancy, 'I really think we ought to move.'

'Nonsense, dear,' called Auntie Bea.

At that, the island gave a bigger shudder and a heave. It felt as if they were going over a hump-bridge in a car. And everything was different.

There was a strong wind. They were all kneeling or standing on very short grass, shivering. There were no trees. Teddy was hanging in the air above Auntie Bea's hut. They could hear the sound of waves crashing all round in the distance, from which they could tell they were on another, bigger island. But they had no idea where.

Almost at once, a hot man in a beret came panting up the green slope towards them. He was wearing a brown sweater with green patches on the elbows and shoulders. 'I say!' he shouted. 'You lot can't picnic here! You're right in the middle of a gun-range there!'

The umbrella heaved. Auntie Bea appeared, looking larger than ever. She had her skirt round her neck like a poncho. 'Don't talk nonsense, my good man,' she said. The soldier stared at her, and at Teddy hanging

over her head. He gave a sort of swallow. 'We leave here over my dead body,' said Auntie Bea, and dived back inside her hut.

'That's just what it will be — ' the soldier started to say, when the island once more tried to shake them off — if that was what it was doing. There was a jerk, and they were on a small rock in the middle of a lake.

'People don't order me about,' Auntie Bea remarked from inside her hut.

There was another jerk, and they were somewhere dark, with water heaving nearby. Honey began to shiver.

'We're having a lovely day!' Auntie Bea asserted, from behind the umbrella.

The island jerked again, quite angrily, and it was freezing cold, but light enough to see by. There was frost or ice under their bare knees. The frosty space was rather small, and heaving, as if it was floating. The sea was very near, dark green, in frighteningly big waves.

'This is an iceberg,' said Nancy, with her teeth chattering. 'That's cheating.'

'How many more kinds of island are there?' shivered Simon. 'No, don't tell me. You'll put ideas in its head. Good dog, Honey.'

'Oh!' Debbie shrieked. 'Teddy's gone! I want to go home. Teddy!'

Auntie Bea, shielded from the ice by her blanket and screened from the view by her hut, called out, 'Don't spoil our lovely day by screaming, dear.'

The iceberg jerked, a bob of annoyance. They were on ice still, but this time it was the top of a mountain. Instead of water, they were surrounded by clouds.

'Teddy!' cried Debbie.

'Lovely day,' repeated Auntie Bea.

Another jerk instantly flung them into sweltering heat, somewhere low down and steamy. Water bubbled between their toes and brown water slid past a few feet away. Honey growled and Nancy gasped. An unmistakable alligator slid by with the water.

'I agree with Debbie,' said Nancy. 'I want to go home.'

'Can't we shut Auntie Bea up?' Simon whispered. 'She keeps annoying it.'

'You'll feel better when you're in the water, dears,' Auntie Bea called out.

Nancy was still shouting, 'No!' when they were pitched somewhere cooler, crowded among bushes under a tall tree. There seemed to be a river in front of them, and park railings beyond that. A banana skin heavily fell on Simon's head. He looked up to find that the tree was full of interested monkeys. Several of them came down to inspect Auntie Bea's hut.

To Simon's amazement, a small boy was staring at them through the railings. 'Hey, Mum,' said the small boy. 'Can I have a picnic on there, too?'

'I want to go home, too,' Simon said uncomfortably.

Two of the monkeys had decided that Auntie Bea's umbrella was fun. They tried to take it up the tree with them. Auntie Bea's hand appeared round the edge of it, slapping.

'Don't be so impatient, dears. I'm nearly ready.'

The monkeys had barely time to chitter angrily, before that island tossed them aside, too. Auntie Bea's hut was suddenly in the middle of a neat flowerbed. Debbie was rolling in red geraniums. There was a great deal of noise all round, but it was not water. It sounded like traffic. Simon jumped to his feet. He was on a mound surrounded by cars and lorries. Faces were pressed against the windows of a passing bus, staring at him.

'We're on a traffic island now,' he said. 'In the middle of a roundabout.'

Nancy stood up, too. 'What will it think of next? I say, Honey's not here!'

'Ready, dears,' called Auntie Bea. She stood up out of her hut in her bathing suit. Simon was gazing round for Honey, but even he was distracted by the sight. Auntie Bea was gigantic. The flowers looked pale beside her. She was like an enormous beachball, only brighter than a beachball has any right to be. The people going by in cars could not take their eyes off her. The bus ran into the kerb. Two cars drove up on to the flowerbeds. Brakes squealed and metal clanged all round the roundabout.

Only Debbie was not distracted by the sight. She was fond of bright colours. 'This is the roundabout at the end of our road!' she said.

'Quick!' said Nancy.

'Run!' said Simon. 'Before she says anything.'

They raced down among the flowers. Behind them, Auntie Bea hooted, 'I do think cars should be banned on beaches,' and vanished from sight — which caused a further pile-up of cars.

Nancy, Simon and Debbie dodged between the cars and ran on, up their road and into their own house.

'Why are you back so soon?' asked Mrs Pearson. She did not seem to have gone to the dentist. 'Where's Auntie Bea?'

She could not understand what had happened. All Debbie could think of was Teddy, last seen floating in the air over a soldier. All Simon could think of was Honey, last seen growling at an alligator. All Nancy could think of was that she was never going near another island — of any kind — as long as she lived. Neither Mr nor Mrs Pearson grasped that something truly odd had happened, until the phone began to ring.

The first caller was very polite and very high up in the Army. They had Teddy, he said, on an island somewhere in Scotland. Could any of the Pearsons please reveal the secret formula that made Teddy float in the air? Was it anything to do with the strawberry juice Teddy was soaked in? When nobody could tell him what made Teddy float, the high-up man said that it certainly had military importance, and would Debbie mind if they kept Teddy for analysis? They would send a new teddy.

'I want *my* Ted!' Debbie shouted, but the Army said it was impossible.

The next person to phone was a Swiss Mountain Guide, who had found the beachball on top of a mountain, complete with the label giving their address. He asked if they wanted it back. They never did answer that, because a policeman called just then, looking rather grim and asking to speak to Auntie Bea. She had caused a Breach of the Peace, he said, and left her radio in the middle of Silas Street roundabout. But nobody, of course, knew where Auntie Bea was by then.

Almost straight away, there was a puzzled phone-call from Iceland. A trawler captain had found a bag of Pearson sweaters floating on an iceberg and wondered if there were any survivors from the wreck. Mr Pearson had just sorted that one out when someone telephoned all the way from South America. His English was not very good, but he seemed to be saying that the water had ruined the battery in the electric torch. But he wanted to assure them that the buckets and spades were quite safe and very useful.

'Ask about Honey,' said Simon.

But the person in South America had not seen a dog, nor even a satisfied-looking alligator.

'Where's Auntie Bea, though?' Mrs Pearson kept asking.

It was soon clear that Auntie Bea was still travelling. The Foreign Office phoned next. There was, they said, a mysterious complaint from the Russian Embassy. A basket full of jelly and sand in yoghurt cups, with the Pearsons' address on it, had somehow appeared on the conning-tower of a Russian submarine. The Russians were holding it for analysis. The Foreign Office wanted to know if they would find anything important in the yoghurt cups.

'I don't think so,' said Mrs Pearson weakly. 'They – they didn't find my sister as well, did they?'

But Auntie Bea had not been heard of. Nor had she been seen by an excited lady in Greece, who phoned next. This lady wanted the Pearsons to know that she was not so poor that she could not find two dozen hard-boiled eggs for herself, thank you. And she was throwing away the bag of clothes. They were too big for anyone on the island. She rang off before anyone could try to explain.

The American Embassy rang next. Auntie Bea's umbrella had been found in the sea off Honolulu. They wondered if Auntie Bea had been drowned. So did the Pearsons. But since the next two calls were from Sweden and Japan, it began to look as if Auntie Bea was still being jerked from island to island.

Quite late that night, the London Zoo phoned. 'It's taken us all this time to trace you,' they said, rather injured. 'The address fell off on our monkey-island. How did you come to leave your dog there, anyway? The monkeys were trying to play with the puppies.'

Mr Pearson said – a little wildly – that he could explain everything. Then he found that the Zoo wanted him to collect Honey and her six new puppies at once. They were in the Children's Zoo. Simon was greatly relieved. He went with his father to fetch Honey, and did not mind in the least when Honey was car-sick, though Mr Pearson did.

Meanwhile the others were still answering the

telephone, and there was still no news of Auntie Bea. They forgot what a trial Auntie Bea had been and became worried. They had tender, troubled thoughts about where she could be. Nancy feared she was marooned on a desert island like Robinson Crusoe, all alone in her bathing suit. Debbie said she was somewhere where they spoke quite another language. Mrs Pearson wrung her hands and said she *knew* Bea was in China, under arrest.

Three days later, Auntie Bea rang up herself. 'You'll never guess, Tom!' she hooted. 'I'm in the Bahamas. I've no idea how I got here, and I've had to borrow money for the phone. You needn't bother to come and get me, Tom. I can manage.'

Mr Pearson thought of all the phone calls, and Debbie still in tears about Teddy and – very crossly – about Honey sick in his clean car. 'I'm glad you can manage, Bea,' he said. 'Come and see us when you get home.' And he rang off.

The Big Sunday Afternoon Bang

Helen Cresswell

What Sunday afternoons needed was a big bang, and this Sunday the children were determined that there should be one.

It was Peter's idea. He was the eldest, though not always the one who had the best ideas. Emma, who was two years younger, had good ideas, too. (It had been her idea to turn the yard into a roller skating rink, for instance, and charge the other kids to come in.) But Peter had a more scientific brain than either Emma or Daisy (who, being only five, could hardly be expected to have a scientific brain, yet).

'This afternoon,' he told Emma on the way back from Sunday School, 'we're really going to shake things up.'

'Are we?' Emma was interested, all right, but still not properly into the Sunday afternoon feeling of desperation and boredom. She was wearing her best green embroidered smock and was watching her black patent shoes flash in and out under its hem. She was also still being Sunday School teacher's pet – which she certainly was. This was not her fault. She happened to like stories, and Bible ones were as good as any others.

'It could be dangerous,' Peter said. 'It's an experiment.'

'All right,' she agreed absently. 'We'll do it.'

By the time dinner was over she was ready, as usual, for anything. Sunday afternoons, the children agreed, were truly awful. It was almost as if something actually happened to make time stop – if anything, it seemed to go backwards. On Sunday afternoon their parents went to sleep. They did not call it sleeping. They called it 'having five minutes' – which anyone could see was wrong. Their mother actually went up and lay on the bed. Their father, after a look at the paper, sank back in the armchair and shut his eyes. Usually, he snored.

This particular Sunday was in June, and it was sunny. This meant that they were allowed in the garden as long as they did not play games, and kept their voices down to whispers. (This was because the Westbys, who lived next door, had 'five minutes', too.)

'What we're going to do,' Peter told them, in the corner of the rockery, behind the laurel, 'is make an explosion!'

The other two stared. Daisy did not even know what an explosion was. Emma did, and felt bound to be cautious.

'How do we know it won't blow *us* up?' she asked. This seemed the most important question to ask.

'We don't,' he replied. 'It's an experiment to make the most almighty bang that'll wake everybody up for miles around. We're going to mix up things that I don't suppose anyone's ever mixed up before, and we don't know *what'll* happen. All I'm saying is, I *hope* it'll go off with a bang!'

'I want to mix,' said Daisy instantly. Mixing was one of her favourite things to do.

'What kind of things are we going to mix?' Emma asked.

'Anything we can lay our hands on. We'll wait till they're both asleep, and then go back in. If we stand on a kitchen chair, we can get to all those packets and bottles in the cupboard. There's lots of stuff up there – real stuff, from the chemist's.'

'Where will we mix it? What if we blow the house up?'

'I've thought of that,' he said. 'We'll dig a hole, here in the garden, and sink a basin into it, and then mix in that.'

'What *sort* of things, though?' she persisted.

'Oh – mustard, salt, vinegar, washing up liquid, milk, floor polish – anything we can find. There's bound to be some chemicals in some of them, and it'll just be a matter of hitting the right mixture.'

Emma thought. A girl at school had told her only last week that it was dangerous to eat oranges and milk together. She said it curdled in the stomach and made poison. This had sounded very likely to Emma, and so she had stopped taking oranges to school.

'Well – I'm going to!' Peter got up. 'Please yourself!'

There was no choice, really. She was, of course, as much in favour of a big bang as he was. She was just not keen on being blown up herself. But by now the special Sunday quiet had already descended like a blight over the whole neighbourhood. Even the birds were subdued, as if they had been warned of the consequences of loud whistling on a Sunday afternoon.

'Come on, then.' She followed him.

'Let's mix!' agreed Daisy happily, and tailed after them.

They tiptoed into the house. It was depressingly quiet. They could only hear the buzzing of a fly and the sound of their father's snoring from the next room.

'Right!'

Carefully Peter edged a chair across the lino and, standing on it, began to hand down bottles, packets and tins. He fetched down nearly everything off the third shelf. Emma stared at it all, awestruck.

'Boracic,' she read on one packet. 'Bicarbonate of soda. *Should* we, do you think?'

'Not in *here,* idiot! I told you — in the garden. Now go and get some of those little plastic building cup things of Daisy's. We'll tip a bit of everything into each, then take it all out on a tray.'

Once the actual work began, Emma enjoyed it. She measured liquids and powders into the multi-coloured cups. She used a mustard spoon, because it seemed safer. She noticed that Peter was using a soup spoon, shovelling out the ingredients with an abandon that was a little alarming. To keep Daisy quiet, they gave her a bottle of washing up liquid and let her squirt it into a jam jar. She enjoyed this very much and it could not possibly, Emma thought, be dangerous. The first trayful ready, they took it out to the garden.

'Now — where shall we have the hole?'

'Not too near the house,' said Emma instantly.

'Not *too* near,' he agreed. 'Here, look, by the hedge.'

He took the trowel and began to dig out a hole between the hedge and the hollyhocks.

'We'd better have it pretty deep,' he said. 'You keep watch and make sure no one's looking.'

Emma stared about her. The gardens were quiet. She looked up at her mother's curtained window, then at the Westbys'. There was no sign of life anywhere. The whole world, it seemed, was having 'five minutes'. Daisy was making a hole of her own, using a spoon.

'Right!' said Peter at last. Carefully he fitted a plastic mixing bowl into the hole. He picked up two of the little cups, hesitated, then threw the contents in. Emma gasped. He carried on, tipping things in and then stirring with a long stick. He paused.

'Nothing's happened.' Emma did not know whether to be pleased or sorry.

'Not likely to,' he said. 'That was only the dry stuff. It's when we start putting the liquids in that things'll start to happen.'

He took a yellowish liquid – cough mixture? – leaned well back from the hole, and threw it in. They waited, then bent over and looked.

'It certainly looks horrible,' said Emma. 'Ugh – and can you smell it?'

A thought struck her.

'Could it turn into poison gas, do you think?'

'Could,' he said. 'Better keep back as much as we can. Lucky we're outside. People only really get overcome by fumes inside.'

All the time Peter was stirring in the liquids, Emma's heart was thudding. She thought how brave he was, crouching there over that foreign, unpredictable mixture. Then everything had gone. They waited.

'I don't think there's going to be an explosion,' said Emma at last.

They sat there. Had it not been a Sunday afternoon, they might even have left it at that. But it was, and teatime was still light years away. The gardens lay deserted under the hot sun.

'Come on!' Peter sprang up. 'There's lots more stuff left to try. We'll hit the right mixture, sooner or later!'

After that a kind of madness took hold of them. They went into the pantry and took some of nearly everything, from currants to tomato sauce. Emma even broke an egg into the hole. It floated on the evil brown mixture like a wicked yellow eye. After that she became giggly, because it seemed to her that what they were making now was a kind of omelette – and omelettes do not blow up.

Peter simply became silent. He was absolutely absorbed, intent on explosion. He still believed that it would come, in the end. 'It won't *half* be a bang,' he muttered, now and again. '*Won't* there be a bang!'

On one of his trips back from the house he actually brought a whole tin of something with him.

'Stand back,' he ordered. '*This'll* do it!'

Emma did not obey him as she would have done earlier. She merely watched with interest as he spooned a great heap of white power into the brownish liquid in the bowl.

'Ooooeeeeh!'

Emma's scream was so loud and long that she actually heard it herself, and clapped her hands over her ears to shut it out. She ran then, towards the house, still screaming and still seeing that awful foaming, seething mass.

'What — what the — ?' Her father was there, redfaced and dazed and already furious. Peter came up beside her, the tin still in his hands.

'Idiot!' he hissed. 'It was only fizzy liver salts!'

'Look!' It was Daisy speaking, from the pantry. They looked. Emma screamed again. Daisy was covered in blood.

It was not blood at all, as it turned out. It was tomato sauce. It was all over the pantry floor as well, and so were a whole bag of flour, a couple of packets of tea and a lot of sugar and gravy salt. Here and there floated the evil yellow eyes of eggs.

'I mixed,' said Daisy happily.

Then their parents were both there, both bad-tempered from so rude an interruption of their 'five minutes' — both, in fact, livid.

Emma and Peter exchanged glances. There *was* going to be an explosion that Sunday, after all . . .

The Dinner Lady Who Made Magic

Dorothy Edwards

Frogover Road Primary School is housed in an old and ugly building. It has windows that are too high to look out of, a yard like iron that you daren't fall down on, bogs that always need plumbing, and more wild kids than good books. There is so much noise coming in from outside, where there is a busy road one way and a railway line the other, that it is murder when the windows have to be wedged open in summer. In winter, when the windows are shut tight, it is like hell, getting hotter and hotter all the time. There was a time when the boilers that clattered and bumbled from below sounded as if they were just going to blow up. That was the time when the school was a pretty dreadful place to be in.

In those days, the Frogover Road kids were a really nasty lot. They pinched one another's dinner money to buy stink bombs to drop at Assembly, they wrote rude things about the teachers in school chalk on the outside walls and blamed other people when they were caught, and they told lies and used swear words and few of them ever spoke below a shout.

The tough kids were always making new gangs and

busting up the old ones and, when that happened, there'd be blacks and whites and Asians and Chinese and Cypriots and Arabs all mixed up, bashing each other up and down the playground and over the classrooms; boys and girls punching and clawing, teachers yelling and screaming at them to stop, and the little tiddlers in the Reception class crying and wanting to go home. As for the kids who weren't tough – they'd just keep out of everyone's way as much as possible, and pretend to read books with their fingers in their ears. The only thing no one ever did at that school was learn anything.

At dinner time, the dinner ladies were as cross as two sticks: they dunked out the potatoes and sloshed the stew and pushed out the plates of prunes and custard without looking anyone in the face, and, as soon as another job came their way, they gave in their notices at once. And the children were so horrible and the teachers so bad-tempered that no one even noticed when they went.

And it might have gone on like that: on and on for ever and ever, getting worse and worse, if it hadn't been for a bit of magic.

Now, you'd never have believed that any kind of magic would have been likely to find its way into that part of London. All those miserable treacherous pavements with the cracks and dips in them, and the houses with several families jammed together under one roof, and the shops with windows full of ugly posters, and the old men who spat at the street corners. 'Magic?' you'd have said. 'Why, even the colour tellies in the hireshop windows aren't magic any more — everyone has them now.'

But there *was* a bit of magic all right. It came over from the West Indies with a boy called Gerry's grandmam. This boy called Gerry's grandmam flew over for a visit one summer and man, was *she* something special? She was a real witch. Nothing creepy or turning you into something horrible if you upset her or anything — just an old black lady who was good at spells. She knew about things: what spices to mix together, the right knots to tie in pig's chitterlings, how many black chicken's feathers to burn at one go, and why you couldn't brew spells over a gas-ring — things like that. Mild stuff for making the odd friendly spell.

Gerry's grandmam was so black that she shone, and so fat that she walked with a bounce like an air-balloon, and so kind that the meanest, crossest checkout girl in the dingiest supermarket had to smile with her. And when she laughed, which she often did, her chuckles gurgled and bubbled like a Lakeland beck and everyone around laughed to hear her.

Now, around the time Gerry's grandmam was over, there was a crisis at Frogover Road, a *serious* crisis – a walk out. There had been trouble in the dinner-hour, real trouble. It had started when a girl called Lucy Wilkins, who had yellow hair with green slides in it, had pushed in front of a girl called Carmen Melinski and tried to take her place in the dinner queue.

Lucy was a big 'I'm-the-boss-lady-around-here' sort of girl, with a strong gang behind her, who liked and expected to be treated as Queen of the School. Carmen was a new girl, little and quiet, with black hair and deep blue eyes and very red lips, who looked like she couldn't blow fluff off a milkshake. No one had expected Carmen to be anything but meek but instead, quick as a flash, Carmen's olive fingers dug themselves into Lucy's gold mop, the green slides skittered to the floor, Lucy fell hard against Horace Loss, a pale-brown West Indian with long eyelashes and a quick temper, and before you could say 'battle' they were all at it. Mashed potato flew across the hall, creamed carrots slithered beneath the struggling bodies, and custard dripped from the table-tops. And then five terrified little first-years, running for refuge among the alarmed dinner ladies, upset the fish fingers on to the stove and caught them alight!

If the school secretary hadn't phoned at once for the police and the fire brigade someone might have been killed. The hot, food-plastered children stood in disgraced rows while first the police sergeant, then the fire chief, and then the Headmistress gave them good tellings off. By rights they should have been sent home in disgrace but, as most of their mothers were working, they'd have had nowhere to go and might have got into more trouble. So there they had to stay, dinner-bedecked and depressed, until it was time for school to finish for the day. The only ones who went home, at once and for ever, were the angry dinner ladies, who resigned in a bunch.

'And now what shall we do?' the school secretary asked the Headmistress.

The Headmistress rang the Chief Education Officer. 'What *shall* we do about dinners in future for Frogover Primary? We can manage with one lady short if we have to, but not the lot. Oh, my!'

But all the Chief Education Officer could say was, 'Advertise, advertise!'

So, whether they liked it or not, the best that could be done for Frogover Road's midday meal was bread and cheese and apples, which made the kids mutinous and their parents ask what they were supposed to be paying for. But what else could be done? Dinner ladies don't grow on trees! The word had gone round and so, in spite of the advertisements that the Headmistress put in the local paper, and the ones that the school secretary placed on the paper-shop boards, and in spite of the phone calls to the Job Centre, no one wanted to work in a school with a reputation as bad as Frogover Road's.

So it went on being bread and cheese cut into lumps by the overworked secretary, and specky apples from the market, and no one daring to grumble aloud because they knew they'd gone too far. What with that Carmen Melinski behaving like a smug mouse, and a thankful gang of previously persecuted nonentities going home in a posse, and Lucy Wilkins with sticking plaster down the side of her face where she had been scratched smouldering in the middle of her lot, and Horace Loss and his mates sulking all playtime down by the dustbins, and Achmed, Shemsha and Mouki and their crowd going off into corners and whispering, it's a wonder that the secretary didn't walk out too.

But she was a nice lady — worried, but nice. The kids quite liked her. One or two of the better-natured ones even felt sorry for her, sorry enough to help with the cheese cutting. But of course it couldn't go on. The situation was explosive.

The third morning after the walk-out of the dinner ladies, while she was waiting at Tesco's check-out with a trolley full of cut loaves and cheese, the harassed school secretary looked across at the queue opposite and saw a face. If the sun had been black, that was how it would have beamed! Springy grey curls under a hat like a crown of coloured veils bobbed and nodded above a broad and all-encompassing smile.

'Don' look so down, secretary Miss,' said Gerry's grandmam, who knew the secretary by sight, for wasn't her grandson a second-year Frogover Roader? 'Seems to me now those children have been punished enough. Too much misery can lead to real bad doings. It's time something nice happened in that miserable old school for a change.'

They met as soon as they had passed through the check-outs, and the school secretary told Gerry's grandmam what was in her heart: all about how old the school was and how crowded and noisy, how the teachers were edgy and how there wasn't even a proper dining room, only the assembly hall with temporary tables down the middle. 'It's not the children, really,' she said. 'It's Things. But you can't blame the dinner ladies either,' she went on. 'Those children were very, very naughty. Do you know, the caretaker says that little bits of dried potato are still dropping off the light bulbs?'

Gerry's grandmam listened, and then she laughed, so that the secretary laughed too, and so did the other

shoppers, and even the passers-by in the High Street who couldn't hear through the glass found themselves smiling as they hurried by.

'I'm having a fine holiday in this old U.K.,' the witch-grandmam said. 'I've been to Brighton, and Buckingham Palace, the Commonwealth Institute and the Oval and to visit my sister and her family in Birmingham. But I ain't never been in a school. So, I'll tell you what, I'll come and help with those dinners for a week or two before I fly home again. That *will* be something to talk about when I get back! And I'll look around and find a couple or so other folk to help me.'

And that's what happened. That evening Gerry's grandmam went down to the fried chicken take-away and talked to a couple of rather posh little old white sister-ladies who were waiting for potato fritters, and somehow these old ladies found themselves offering to help out as dinner ladies.

'It's an emergency – like in the war time,' said one. 'I remember making cocoa for the air raid wardens.'

'We must do our bit for the children,' said the other, and they giggled with pleasure.

Gerry's grandmam knew a girl called Winnie Wong who sat about all day painting her nails, so she called and asked her if she'd like to help in the school kitchen as a change from nail-painting and idling. And, although she'd never meant to, somehow Winnie Wong found herself saying, 'Yes, all right.'

'Three good helpers will be enough, I guess,' that old witch-grandmam said.

That night Gerry's grandmam got busy in the small trodden yard behind the house where Gerry's family lived. On a black skillet over a fire of wood-chips she frizzled feathers and burned spices and whispered spells as old as Africa. With a long iron spoon she stirred and mashed the growing magic, turning it over and over to ensure that every bit received its appropriate incantation, until the fire died and fell away to white ash, and the skillet cooled and all that remained was a bare spoonful of glittery powder.

Next morning at nine o'clock the new dinner helpers arrived: Gerry's grandmam in her magnificent hat and a flowing overall patterned with birds of paradise, the pale old sisters in frilly pink aprons with streamers that had once been worn by a long-ago parlourmaid, and Winnie Wong in the dark blue trousers and tunic of a Chinese worker, with a red carnation tucked behind her ear for luck. There they were, all ready to heat and dish up the school dinners.

For the first time for days a good warm smell rose up from the kitchen and penetrated the classrooms. That day the Central Kitchen had delivered stew, which now bubbled over the gas-rings.

'Hi-yee-ah,' said Gerry's grandmam as she raised the heavy lids and looked down upon the mutton and vegetables. 'Hi-yee-ah,' she said again, and a pinch of something small and glittery and magic slipped from the end of her wooden spoon and was lost to sight as she stirred the pot.

In the meantime, one of the posh old ladies and Winnie Wong put up the tables and arranged the chairs, while the other sister popped out to the market and came back with a couple of bunches of pink daisies which she divided out into empty milk bottles and put on each table. 'There!' she said. 'The children will like those!'

The Frogover kids came eagerly to dinner, their noses twitching. For them, they were fairly quiet. There was a hushed feeling in the air and, as they fell into line, they spoke in whispers.

Gerry's grandmam in her rainbow hat served up the

mouth-watering stew and beamed as each child carried its plate to where Miss Wong waited, her beautiful fluttering pale hands with their painted nails poised to spoon out the mash and lay it delicately and deliciously beside the meat and veg.

The little old ladies, twittering and tottering, wandered round with fresh jugs of water and helped the little ones to cut their meat and offered cubes of bread like dear old-fashioned grannies, speaking so politely in their posh soft voices that the startled children spoke softly if not poshly back.

And, as they ate, the magic worked; it sank into angry stomachs and soothed and petted them into kindness. Querulous teachers suddenly hushed and smiled at each other. Lucy Wilkins peeled off the sticking plaster which she'd only been wearing for effect — for the marks of Carmen's nails had healed days before — and, rolling it neatly, dropped it in her pocket. Horace Loss and his mates, who had recently formed themselves into the Horseshoe Gang, rose as one boy and, without being asked, collected the empty plates of the Reception class, and fetched the helpings of jam roll to save the little things from having to queue. And the Asian children, who were mostly vegetarians, smiled at everyone for, although they had not tasted the stew themselves, the magic working away inside everyone else had created a friendliness they were only too pleased to share.

After dinner, Gerry's grandmam and her helpers washed up and stacked away the dishes, singing happily together. The blended voices of the witch-grandmam, the posh old ladies, and the lovely Winnie Wong filled the school as pleasantly as the scent of the midday stew and the kids and the teachers smiled as they listened, and then went on with the lessons in the smoothest way imaginable.

So, day after day, until it was time for her to fly home, Gerry's grandmam and her helpers served the school dinners, dispensing magic until the miserable old building became bright and colourful, the outside noises sounded as pleasant as early morning bird songs, and the rumbles of the downstairs boiler seemed like the drowsy chuckles of a slumbering giant. Now the school was talked about as a place in a million. Somewhere where it was good to be. Somewhere where the kids liked learning and the teachers liked teaching.

News of its transformation spread through the

neighbourhood. In a body, just as they had walked out, the dinner ladies returned to plead for their old jobs back. By now the magic had truly worked. It had penetrated every crack and cranny of the old school building and soaked into the hearts of all who entered it. The Headmistress knew that it would soon be time for Gerry's grandmam to go back home, and that the posh old sisters would be leaving to join the W.V.S., and that Winnie Wong was soon to marry Mr Ah Foo from the Chinese diner, and so she graciously welcomed the dinner ladies back. And now, so good were the children and so pleasant the teachers, that the dinner ladies found themselves beaming as they dished out the dinners.

Before she left, Gerry's grandmam gave the chief dinner lady a small tinful of magic. 'Just drop a bit in now and again,' she said. 'You may as well use it up.'

But the chief dinner lady didn't believe in spells and she threw the tin away next day. It didn't really matter, though, for the magic had done its work and goes on making things better and better. When the time comes for those kids to grow up and make their own lives among those old streets and houses, they'll have so much magic in them that they'll make the place a paradise!

A Ghost of One's Own
Ursula Moray Williams

Harriet was in the bus, on her way to a party, carrying her family ghost in a basket. She was going to see Miss Meadie, who was giving the party at her home. Her brother William sat on the seat opposite to her, looking sulky, because he had not wanted to come.

Some people can see ghosts and some cannot. Harriet, alone of all her family, could. Her brother William could not, but he could feel them and hear them. And he could smell them, for some ghosts have a fragrance very like old herbs and roses. William did not care for ghosts, so this caused him a lot of inconvenience.

The rest of the family just did not believe in them at all. So they would not be likely to take any notice of the advertisement in a column of the local paper that said: 'All Ghosts Welcome at Miss Meadie's Party on Friday Next.' It did not say who Miss Meadie was, nor where she lived, but anyone who really wanted to go to the party could surely find out.

Harriet had found out long ago, before she had a ghost of her own, when she was riding her bicycle back from school and had turned aside to explore the driveway of an old country estate. Harriet recognised it at once as ghost territory, even before she met Miss Meadie coming down the drive carrying armfuls of freshly-cut phantom roses which could not possibly be real, since it was February. There was a ghost dog at her heels, and a real one, and two semi-invisible cats, also an old butler, who looked at Harriet and vanished.

Miss Meadie recognised Harriet at once as a Ghost Believer. She gave her a rose and invited her to tea.

'You must come and visit me whenever you like!' Miss Meadie told her. 'And bring your friends with you. I mean your personal friends, of course, not your flesh-and-blood ones. I know just what it is like to have your dear ones snubbed and slighted and ignored and not believed in. You must bring them to me instead!'

Harriet was too embarrassed to explain that she had no phantom of her own at present. True, she saw and heard other people's wherever she went, but they all belonged to someone else.

'You do have a ghost of your own, I suppose?' Miss Meadie said sharply, and for a moment Harriet felt that she had arrived under false pretences.

She saved herself by saying calmly: 'Well, just at present I haven't got one, but my brother William has a skeleton.'

'A skeleton?' said Miss Meadie with interest. 'And why has he not come to see me?'

'My brother,' Harriet explained, 'doesn't like ghosts!'

'Doesn't *like* them?' Miss Meadie repeated. 'But they are lovely things! So gentle! So affectionate . . . so beautiful! Why doesn't your brother William think that ghosts are beautiful?'

'My brother can't *see* ghosts,' Harriet explained. 'He can only hear and feel them. It makes it difficult for him. But he found the skeleton in the loft, himself, and although he can't see it he seems very fond of it. It goes everywhere with him, except to school. It is a very quiet

skeleton, only sometimes it has some mischievous ways. It trips up my father in the hall when William leaves it around. My father does not believe in ghosts at all.'

'So sad!' said Miss Meadie. 'So sad!'

'I must be going now,' said Harriet.

'Very well,' said Miss Meadie. 'Come back when you have a ghost of your own.'

Harriet felt that she had fallen short of Miss Meadie's expectations. The parting was a little cold. But she had no idea where she could get a ghost for herself. You couldn't buy them, and William's had arrived quite by accident, due to rummaging in the loft on a wet day in the holidays. As far as Harriet was concerned, he was welcome to it. She did not care for skeletons, but since meeting Miss Meadie she had realised that just seeing ghosts was not enough for a true ghost lover. One ought to have a phantom of one's own.

She did, quite soon.

Harriet and William lived in one half of a semi-detached Victorian villa. The baby belonging to the people in the other half cried all night long, but when their mother mentioned it to the baby's mother she was most indignant, and said that the baby slept in her room and never woke up all night, ever.

'I didn't hear it myself. It was the children who mentioned it,' Harriet's mother said, apologising hastily.

The next time the baby cried, Harriet took a torch, woke her brother William, and climbed the stairs to the loft. There was a thin partition between their part of the loft and the next-door part. The baby was crying on the other side. Harriet made a hole in the partition, clambered through, and found the baby lying in an old-fashioned basket cradle. The moment it saw her, it stopped crying and smiled.

It was a lovely fat ghostling baby. William, shining the torch for Harriet, could not see it at all, but he was forced to admit it was there when Harriet thrust its warm, curly head against his fingers. She carried it downstairs to her room, and cuddled it and loved it and thought of little else for days and days. Sometimes she fed it on bread and milk, but ghost babies do well enough living on air.

Now she had her baby ghost and William had his skeleton. Their mother could not make them out at all.

'My children have almost *too* much imagination!' she complained to her friends. 'They play all day long with imaginary companions! Harriet pretends she is looking after a baby! She pushes it out in an old doll's pram that she hasn't looked at for years. She is really much too big to push a doll's pram. And William carries round a polythene shopping bag as if there was something precious inside it! Perhaps they are geniuses! I don't know!'

So here they were, going to Miss Meadie's party by bus, since it was difficult to take either the baby or the skeleton on a bicycle, and William was a little sulky because he had not wanted to go, but Harriet had persuaded him it would be hard luck on the skeleton if he didn't.

Harriet had been to visit Miss Meadie just once more, after she had found the baby.

'Good!' said Miss Meadie. 'It is just in time to come to my ghost party.'

Harriet stared.

'I give a ghost party every year,' Miss Meadie went

on. 'On Hallowe'en, of course! The patrons like it and it keeps the ghosts off the streets. You can come!'

'And William?' asked Harriet.

'If that is the skeleton boy, then of course he can come,' said Miss Meadie. 'But don't tell all and sundry. I only want people *with* ghosts, not people without, and I don't want newspapermen or the general public. They might win the game and that would be a pity.'

'What game?' asked Harriet at once.

'Why, the Wishing Bean game!' said Miss Meadie. 'The darling ghosties look forward to it all the year round. You see, after everybody has eaten all they can, I bring on a great dish of hot spiced curry, very hot and very spicy, and somewhere in it there is hidden a little round yellow bean. Everybody eats and eats and eats in the hope that the bean will be found in their portion, because if it is . . .'

'What?' asked Harriet, excited.

'They have a wish!' said Miss Meadie. 'And the wish comes true. Always. Just that one wish, at that one moment in the year.'

'What do they usually wish for?' asked Harriet, wondering what a ghost could desire on such an occasion.

'You never can tell!' said Miss Meadie, shaking her head. 'The very strangest things! There was a cavalier — you know, the kind of fellow who carries his head under his arm. We were all so pleased when he got the bean. We felt sure he would wish to have his head put back on his shoulders again. Well, wouldn't you? But not a bit of it! He wished for a really dashing hat with white feathers in it! He said he would be able to admire it much more easily if he wore it underneath his arm.'

'What else did they wish for?' asked Harriet.

'Well, there was a lady who had been drowned,' said Miss Meadie. 'She wished for a modern permanent wave, because they did not have them in her day. But sometimes it isn't the ghosties who get the bean. Sometimes it's the patrons, and some are very selfish. They wish for cruises in the Mediterranean and things like that which their dear ones can't take part in. One of them wanted a flat in Paris. His ghost couldn't go *there* — it couldn't understand French! So selfish, wasn't it?'

'Can they wish for just anything?' asked Harriet.

'Just anything!' said Miss Meadie. 'And when I think of all the wasted opportunities, I sometimes think I'll never give a party again.'

Harriet immediately began to think what she would wish for if she got the bean at Miss Meadie's party, and she decided on a really beautiful perambulator for the baby, that she could push around without being told that she was really too old for a doll's pram.

'I think it is very kind indeed of you to give a party for us and our ghosts,' she told Miss Meadie. 'Everyone must be very grateful to you.'

'Well, we have our enemies, of course,' said Miss Meadie. 'No doubt you read the advertisement in the paper under the heading "Miscellaneous"?'

Harriet had not. Miss Meadie handed her the paper.

' "Let me solve your psychic problems",' Harriet read aloud. 'Is it advertising medicine?'

'*Psychic,* not *physic!*' said Miss Meadie, fondling the two ghost cats that were sparring for her attention. 'Read on!'

' "Exorciser guarantees to rid you of pests, blackbeetles and all unnatural phenomena for a moderate fee. Apply: Rid-a-Ghoster, Telephone 0000007. All correspondence answered." '

'How silly!' said Harriet. 'I bet he can't do it!'

'Don't be too sure,' said Miss Meadie. '*We* love our ghosties, so they are safe with us, but hatred is very dangerous. It destroys. And I don't believe that Mr Rid-a-Ghoster is a true exorcist or he wouldn't do it for money. A real exorcist helps our friends into another world with love and tenderness, if they really want to go. *He* does it with their consent and co-operation. This man is just out to make money.'

'Well, he shan't have *my* little ghost, or William's!' said Harriet firmly.

The bus shook and jolted. William's skeleton got out of the bag and sat beside him on the seat, since there were very few passengers. The baby slept contentedly in Harriet's basket. She kept peeping at it to see if it was awake or not.

'What have you got in there, love?' asked the woman sitting next to her. 'Is it a kitten?'

'No,' said Harriet, going red.

'Is it a bunny, then?'

'No!' said Harriet, furious with herself for having made loving noises to the baby ghost. 'It's nothing at all!' she added firmly.

The lady was too inquisitive to let that pass. She leaned across Harriet as if to peer inside the basket. The baby woke up and cried.

'Look! It's nothing at all!' Harriet repeated defiantly. She thrust the basket under the lady's nose and saw the look of surprise that came into her face when she realised that, in fact, it appeared perfectly empty. William, who had been dozing, woke up with a jerk.

'Why's it crying?' he asked loudly.

The skeleton kicked him.

'Ouch!' William said, rubbing his shin. 'You didn't have to do that! I wish I hadn't brought you!'

The lady sat back, looking perfectly astonished, and the bus, arriving at a bus stop, ground to a halt. William, still rubbing his shin, was avenged when a new passenger sat down solidly on top of his skeleton, though only Harriet could see its indignant limbs sticking out on either side of the tweed-coated gentleman who had almost obliterated it.

And suddenly she noticed that the newcomer himself was not without his attendant sprites. His pockets were full of small poltergeists, busy unpicking his buttons, unravelling his pipe tobacco and making holes in his handkerchief. The man seemed to be only half aware of them, but Harriet could see that he was a worried person.

Before the bus restarted, a cloppetting of hooves down the road brought Harriet's head round with a jerk. A man was running at full speed to catch the bus, holding by a rope an enormous grey mare with fiery eyes and the sort of transparency about it that Harriet had long since learned to associate with phantoms. William looked round too, but when the man had leapt on board he took no further notice. He was stroking the skeleton's hand as it clung to his knee for reassurance. Harriet saw that the horse was attempting to board the bus as well.

'Step along please!' the conductor said, as the man stopped to buy his ticket.

The horse reared up and came down with one of its forefeet fair and square on the conductor's toe. Harriet winced, but the conductor went on punching the ticket as if nothing had happened, and then moved away down the bus, while the man tied the horse's rope to the rail inside the door and sat down on the other side of Harriet, breathing heavily. The horse's hooves pounded along behind, breaking into a gallop as the bus gathered speed.

The horse's owner was staring across at William and William's neighbour as if his eyes would pop out of his head. Harriet realised that the man had noticed something, but just how much she could not tell. To test him, she opened the basket, and the baby began to cry. Harriet took it in her arms.

'Cor! Nice little kid!' said the man admiringly, and then, in a tone of relief: 'You going to Miss Meadie's party, then?'

Harriet realised that her neighbour too had the gift of seeing Other Things. She nodded.

'Didn't see you there last year,' the man went on conversationally. 'Is that your brother across the way? He's like you. That chap beside him, what's sitting on all those bones, he's a funny one, he is. He's stark staring terrified of those little tiddlers playing up and down his weskit. He brings 'em every year hoping Miss Meadie will get rid of 'em for him, but she loves 'em, bless her heart. Now I wouldn't mind a snuff-out powder for my horse! He's a right nuisance, kicking his stall to pieces when the moon is full and when hounds go by — well! You can't hold him! He's after 'em, and every dog of 'em puts its tail between its legs and hares for home! No wonder all the foxes run straight for my place! You can see 'em laughing! But the Hunt thinks I does it on purpose.'

'Bad luck!' said Harriet.

'Anyway, I've had enough,' said the man. 'This year I'm getting rid of him. There's a chap coming to Miss Meadie's party that can settle things for good and all. An exorcist, he's called. I believe he's a dab hand at ghosts.'

Harriet was just opening her mouth to say that Miss Meadie would never invite anyone like that to her party, when the bus stopped again, a new passenger got on, and immediately, in front of Harriet's very eyes, every ghost went out like a light.

The baby, which had been kicking and chuckling, began to cry bitterly, and Harriet rocked it to and fro to comfort it.

Opposite, the skeleton somehow eased itself out from beneath the body of the man on top and folded itself back into William's bag. The little poltergeists became as flat as shadows and disappeared inside various pockets. Their patron, who seemed to have even less awareness than William, remained staring straight ahead of him with his hands on his knees, while the newcomer walked quietly to the very front of the bus and sat down. He wore a wide-brimmed black hat, and a long black coat. His ears stuck out slightly, and he had a long, thin nose.

Harriet was acutely aware of something wrong about him. He looked just horrid. The horse-owner suddenly noticed him too.

'That's the bloke!' he muttered to Harriet. 'That's the Rid-a-Ghost man! He's going to do quite a bit of business at the party, he told me. I'm not the only one wanting to get rid of a ghostie. Just look at my old grey mare there! Her's got the message!'

Outside the bus, in fact, the grey mare, with her ears laid flat back against her head, could be seen straining against the rope that pulled her. Faintly at William's feet, the skeleton's teeth could be heard chattering inside the carrier bag.

While the horse's owner moved down the bus to speak confidentially to the uncanny stranger, Harriet noticed that the knot securing the horse's rope to the rail was on the point of coming undone.

'Hold the baby a minute!' she said to William, dumping it on his knees.

'It'll wet,' said William gingerly.

'No, it won't, you twit! It will only feel as if it does!' said Harriet, dashing up the bus. She seized the rope just as the horse was about to break away, and tied it securely to the rail.

'Hey!' shouted the conductor. 'Don't get off before the bus stops!' But the bus was already slowing down.

Nearly everybody got off at the stop nearest to Miss Meadie's. Harriet got off first. She flew up the drive to warn Miss Meadie about the unwelcome visitor who was about to invade the party. But Miss Meadie, busy receiving a score of invited guests, had little time to listen to what Harriet was saying.

Patron after patron, ghost after ghost, were being welcomed into the hall, and shown to their seats at a long table which was piled with all kinds of delicious food. When everyone was in their places, Harriet saw to her great relief that the Rid-a-Ghoster was not, after all, among them. Perhaps his courage had failed him in the face of such a happy throng of friends and phantoms, now raising their glasses to toast Miss Meadie, and drinking to the Past, the Happy Past and the Past Again.

Watching the enthusiasm of ghosts and patrons alike, Harriet found it hard to believe that any of these loyal guests could be planning to jettison their phantom friends before the evening was out. She clutched the ghostling baby more closely to her, and noticed that William and his skeleton were fondly sharing a dish of trifle, and clinking spoons.

The evening passed with feasting and music, the excitement growing more intense as one phantom after another burst into song, and everybody joined in. The horse neighed after every verse, the skeleton danced a fandango on the table, the poltergeists pelted everyone with popcorn and Miss Meadie called them her naughty little piglets.

Then at last she clapped her hands, and silence fell.

'We have now come to the climax of our feast!' announced Miss Meadie. 'I shall bring in the dish of the Wishing Bean. You all know what to do! Each one will serve himself with as large a portion as he is still able to eat, and in one of the portions will be found a small, round bean! Whoever finds it can wish one wish aloud, and that wish is bound to come true. Blessings on you all, and may the lucky one's dreams be realised!'

There was a burst of applause as she rose to leave the table, followed by the phantom butler and several dogs and cats, some quite transparent and others with the normal complement of heads, tails and whiskers. Harriet watched her go with mounting excitement. The great moment of the day had arrived! And everyone, *everyone,* had a chance to win. Even the baby would have to be woken up to taste its portion.

But when she looked back again at the table, the Rid-a-Ghoster was sitting in Miss Meadie's chair. Where he had come from nobody could say, but he did not give them time to wonder.

'Friends!' he shouted, leaping to his feet. 'The fun and games are over! The phantoms have had their day!

Life is not a party for the dead-and-gone-before! Life goes on, tomorrow and the next day and the next, and the one after! Do we want to remain in the thraldom of our hauntings? Do we want to hear again the cryings in the dark, the knockings on the door, the trippings-up and the trippings-in? Do we want our cats' fur standing on end? Our dogs crouching in corners with their tails between their legs? Our plates and cups and saucers hurled about our heads? Do we want to be controlled all our lives long by these wretched manifestations we call ghosts, for want of a better name for them? No! No! Many of you have already come to me for help in ridding you of these pests. Many of you have asked me to meet you here tonight in order to destroy these — these blackbeetles! Pah! But I am your friend! Trust in the Rid-a-Ghoster and you shall be freed from your fears! Five pounds please, paid in advance!'

Harriet sat horrified. She saw some of the patrons looking sheepishly at each other. Two or three put their hands into their pockets, searching for money. A few pound notes were already passing into the Rid-a-Ghoster's greedy palm.

The kitchen door was flung open and Miss Meadie appeared, bearing a steaming dish. She gave one look at the Rid-a-Ghoster and banged the dish down on the table in front of him.

'My seat, if you please,' she said curtly.

Unwillingly, the Rid-a-Ghoster gave it up to her. 'I remain at your service!' he announced to the table at large. 'Whoever wishes to avail themselves of my powers may come with me into the next room. Bring your phantoms with you. Those who have already paid will be served first.'

He was about to retire when he saw that the attention of the whole company was riveted on the

Wishing Dish. Nobody wanted to lose their chance of finding the wonderful bean. Those who wished to be exorcised decided to have it done afterwards.

Reluctantly the Rid-a-Ghoster sat down among the rest, and before he could be prevented, he snatched an ample portion of the dish's contents as it circled the table.

The bean was too small to be seen with the naked eye, but Miss Meadie assured everyone that they would know it when they found it on their tongues.

An atmosphere of intense expectation filled the room. Everybody wanted to find the precious bean, and one could almost see the shadows of the various wishes flitting round the table.

Harriet was terribly anxious. There were at least forty chances to one against her winning the bean. She did not even expect to get it. Supposing William got it? If he were sitting nearer to her she could tell him what to wish for, but that was not allowed.

Suppose the horse got it? Nobody would even know. It had swallowed its portion already, and the bean might have gone down with it as far as anyone could tell. Suppose one of the poltergeists got it? They were bound to do something silly with it — they were that sort of person. Suppose the baby got it? But, after the first mouthful, it went back to sleep and Harriet ate its share herself.

The company chewed on. The hall was very quiet now, everyone glancing covertly at his neighbour, dreading any hesitation that might signal the finding of the bean.

The worst thing that could happen, Harriet decided, was that the Rid-a-Ghoster should get it. He was quite capable of destroying every phantom in the room if he did. He ate with concentration, carefully chewing every mouthful to the end and sometimes looking up to catch Harriet's eye upon him.

'If he gets it,' Harriet thought, 'I know he will get rid of the baby, and I'll never see it again. I couldn't bear it! I'd just die! And Miss Meadie will die, too, if he destroys all the darling ghosts that she loves so much . . .'

Even Miss Meadie was chewing desperately, keeping her eye meanwhile on the Rid-a-Ghost man. She was almost willing him not to find the bean.

All of a sudden, the Rid-a-Ghoster stopped eating, and choked.

The whole table froze, stopped their own chewing, and looked at him. The Rid-a-Ghoster leaned over the table, coughing and spluttering, while the skeleton kindly beat him on the back between the shoulder blades.

The Rid-a-Ghoster searched for a handkerchief in his pocket and put it to his lips.

'He's got it!' Harriet said to herself, feeling quite faint. 'He's got it . . . he's got the bean!'

At that moment her own tongue met something hard inside her mouth. She pushed it impatiently aside and was about to swallow it when the piercing realisation of what it might be, of what it actually *was,* arrested her in the middle of her swallow. Quickly she put her hand to her mouth and removed a tiny, hard round bean from the back of her tongue. Even when she saw it lying in the palm of her hand, she could hardly believe it.

'I've got the bean!' Harriet announced.

Her first feeling was of such pure relief that she wanted to burst into tears. The Rid-a-Ghoster, whatever else he might do, could not now destroy them all. Then all the wishes that she had ever wished for came crowding into her head, wishes for her family, wishes for herself, wishes for other people.

But the wish that came bursting from her lips even before she found words to say it went ringing round the table, and everyone stared and listened, and listened and stared again, as Harriet shouted:

'I wish that all the ghosts in this room were real people for ever and ever and ever!'

A hush fell upon Miss Meadie's table, and one by one each guest looked at one another. Nobody said a word, until the horse's owner got to his feet, remarking: 'That's a good horse, that one is! And I reckon it's about time he carried me home!' He left the room quietly, and they heard him clopping away down the drive.

There came a popping sound from the direction of the gentleman with the poltergeists, followed by another and another, as if small fireworks were exploding. He got up from the table and left, quite alone. There wasn't a sign of anything fussing about in his pockets and he seemed much calmer.

'Exactly!' murmured Miss Meadie, half-aloud. 'I never did understand about poltergeists . . . '

The cavalier with the feathered hat was now a smartly dressed Member of Parliament. He said goodbye to Miss Meadie, explaining that he had to be in the House in the morning. The drowned lady was talking about sailing to someone who had looked very much like a pirate a few moments ago. They were arranging to sail round the world together. A tonsured monk was now a bishop, returning thanks for the meal they had all received, while a small grey lady left early, saying she had duties in the Public Library and would put Miss Meadie's books on psychic research on one side for her to collect in the morning.

The strangest transformation of all was William's skeleton. It had completely disappeared. By William's side was a charming young woman who was cuddling Harriet's baby. 'It is my baby,' she told Harriet. 'It always was. But you can come and play with it whenever you like.'

Harriet realised that this was for the best. A real live baby that everyone could interfere with was much less convenient than a phantom. Besides which, a real live baby would be even more enchanting to play with than a ghostling.

'Do you mind about your skeleton being a *her?'* she asked William.

'No,' he replied. 'If it can't be a skeleton I don't care what it is,' and he turned away.

The Rid-a-Ghoster was escaping through the door when several people prevented him, and took back their money. He did not even have enough left for his bus fare, and had to walk back to the town.

Harriet turned to Miss Meadie. She was feeling very guilty at the ways things had turned out. 'I'm terribly sorry,' she said. 'I seem to have taken away all your friends at once.'

Suddenly she noticed that Miss Meadie herself looked quite different from the Miss Meadie she had known before.

'It doesn't matter,' Miss Meadie said quietly. 'I was really getting tired of being a ghost myself. I'd rather be a human being. I'm going to have a home for cats and dogs that people have deserted. Goodnight, Harriet! I'm glad you won the bean. Come and see me sometimes, and I hope you enjoyed the party.'

And Harriet and William went home by bus, quite alone.